An Adventure in Caribbean Cuisine

EDITORS
Janice Archibald (Chief Editor)
Rabbia Bibi Annief
Olga Britton
Helen Edinboro-Gonsalves
Norma Howard
Norma Washington

CONTRIBUTORS

Antigua and Barbuda	Jennifer Athill Sharon Browne Gwendolyn Tonge
Barbados	Norraine Davis (deceased) Audrey Drayton Veda Gill Mildeane Massiah Samuel Jackman Polytechnic: Eslyn Estwick Ian Gaskin Tricia Greaves Alicia Phillips
Dominica	Joan Severin
Guyana	Rabbia Bibi Annief Janice Archibald Denise Britton-Gordon Omodele Craig Helen Edinboro-Gonsalves Murlin English Thelma Holder-Bess Cecelia Peters Frances Shepherd-Palmer Food Policy Division of Ministry of Health: Simone Downey Kim Fraser Shavon Morris
Jamaica	Versada Campbell
Montserrat	Althea La Rose-Allen
St Croix	Josephine Peterson-Springer
St Kitts and Nevis	Desiree Claxton
St Lucia	Andrena Blaize-Joseph Deborah Desir Priscilla Philip
Trinidad and Tobago	Catherine Cumberbatch

CARIBBEAN ASSOCIATION OF HOME ECONOMISTS

C.A.H.E 1972

HOME ECONOMICS FOR A BETTER CARIBBEAN COMMUNITY

c/o Samuel Jackman Prescod Polytechnic, Wildey, St Michael, Barbados, West Indies
Tel: (246) 426-1920; Ext: 2227 E-mail: info@c-a-h-e.com
Website: www.maxpages.com/cahe or www.c-a-h-e.com

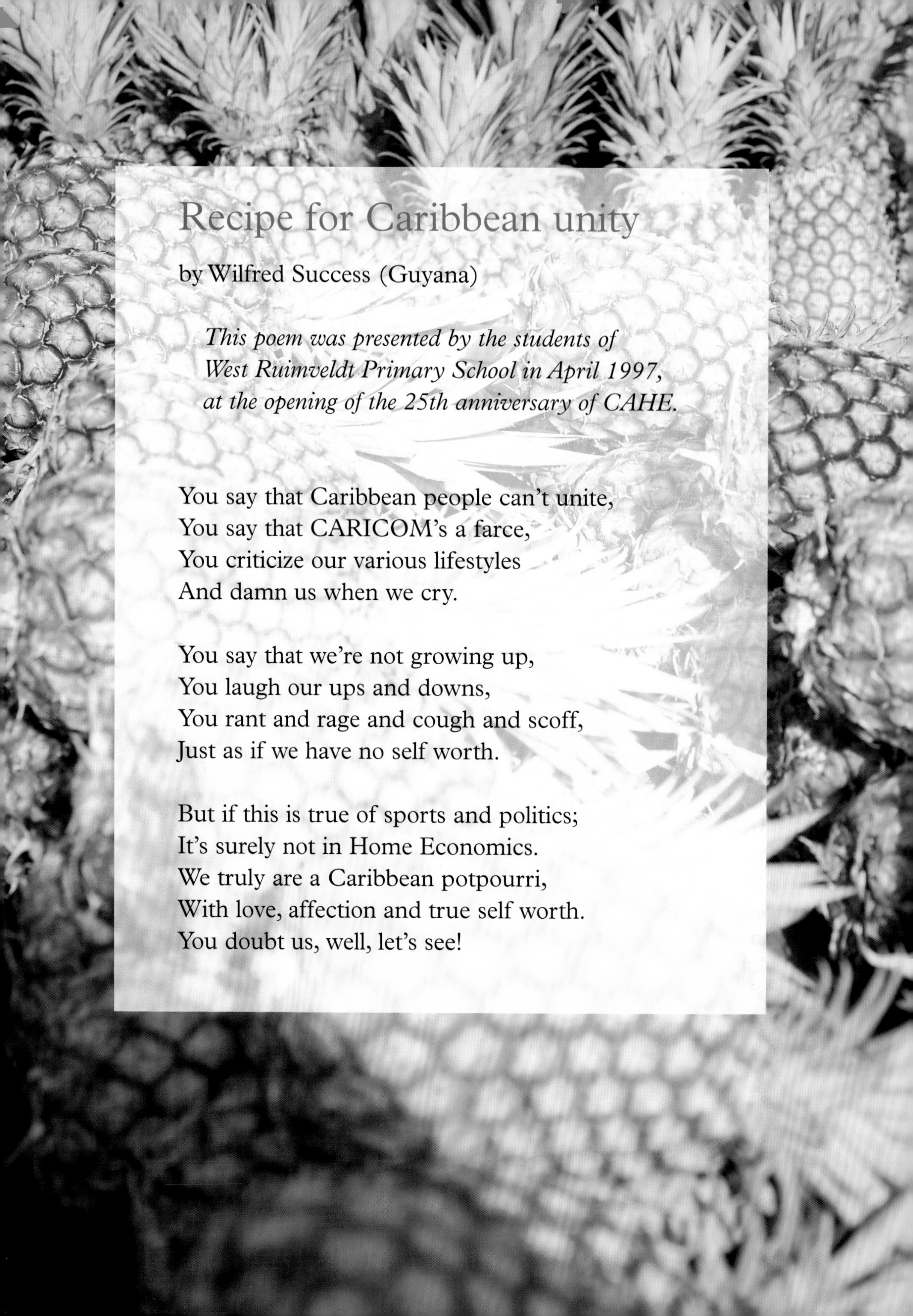

Recipe for Caribbean unity

by Wilfred Success (Guyana)

This poem was presented by the students of West Ruimveldt Primary School in April 1997, at the opening of the 25th anniversary of CAHE.

You say that Caribbean people can't unite,
You say that CARICOM's a farce,
You criticize our various lifestyles
And damn us when we cry.

You say that we're not growing up,
You laugh our ups and downs,
You rant and rage and cough and scoff,
Just as if we have no self worth.

But if this is true of sports and politics;
It's surely not in Home Economics.
We truly are a Caribbean potpourri,
With love, affection and true self worth.
You doubt us, well, let's see!

Ingredients
1 kg of Antiguan patience
1 kg of St Lucian endurance
1 measure of love from Trinidad and Tobago
2 cups of Guyanese hospitality
1 pack of pride from Barbados
2 tbsp of Bahamian pleasure
½ cup of experience from Montserrat
1 cup of determination from Dominica
some mental toughness from St Vincent
spices of hope from Grenada
1 measure of tolerance from Jamaica
1 pinch of Belizean honesty
1 tbsp of generosity from St Kitts
and a little insight from Suriname

And what do we do?

Method
1. Take patience, love and hospitality. Mix together with tolerance, toughness and endurance.
2. Stir well with experience. Add determination and hope.
3. Grill in honesty, sprinkled with generosity.
4. Pour insight, pleasure and pride, beat well with understanding.
5. Place mixture in a pan of purity.
6. Bake in oven of truth with a suitable temperature of tropical sunshine.
7. Cut in a number of slices and serve when cooled.

Serve … to the countries of the Caribbean with water from the Caribbean Sea, and don't forget the Atlantic.

Contents

Foreword

It is a distinct honour and pleasure to recommend to our readership the latest in a series of prominent publications from the Caribbean Association of Home Economists (CAHE), this timely recipe book – *An Adventure in Caribbean Cuisine.*

The project was facilitated through the untiring efforts of an ad hoc committee headed by Mrs Janice Maison, former Research Chair (1993–7), and immediate Past President, CAHE. The input and the collaborative efforts of the CAHE membership in the respective territories is also commendable. It was, indeed, a 'labour of love'.

It is hoped that the tantalizing recipes, useful cooking tips and the general nutrition-related information will provide enjoyable cooking experiences; promote greater mastery of culinary skills; and, by extension, offer valuable insights into the cultures of the peoples of our Caribbean civilization. The importance of this significant educational tool therefore cannot be over-emphasized.

With much pride I endorse this recipe book. I am positive that you, dear reader, will find *An Adventure in Caribbean Cuisine* to be of tremendous value. Happy cooking – and *bon appetit!*

Sonja Lewis
President, CAHE (2005–7)

Preface

'For the Lord thy God bringeth thee into a good land, a land of brooks of water, of fountains and depths that spring out of valleys and hills; a land of wheat, and barley, and vines, and fig trees, and pomegranates; a land of olive oil, and honey' – Deuteronomy 8: 7–8

This compilation of 'Caribbean Cuisine' represents not only a set of traditional dishes but also, more specifically, a collection of original recipes which have been developed by Caribbean home economists from the membership of CAHE, using materials indigenous to the individual territories. Any overlap among the types of food items used is in itself indicative of the merging of cultures over the years as well as the unique heritage of the Caribbean people. This blend of nations has flavoured our dishes significantly in a manner which is no longer specific to any ethnic group but can only be described as 'Caribbean'.

Caribbean foods generally lend themselves to interesting experimentation. Over the last three decades a deep interest has developed among Caribbean chefs and home economists in finding innovative ways of using indigenous foods to create meals to titillate the palate. Response to this book has been rewarding, and it was obvious that some territories accepted the challenge as a way of exploring all possible uses for one specific food. For example, St Lucia provided a range of recipes using the mammee apple (apricot) and the breadnut, Antigua dealt in the same way with the pumpkin; while the team from the Samuel Jackman Prescod Polytechnic in Barbados developed a variety of breads. Other home economists submitted individual recipes from their experiments.

The material within the book is organized to give both background and culinary guidance, as well as information on nutritive value, about the various foods used in the Caribbean. The individual recipes are enhanced by the addition of nutrition information, provided for the whole recipe as well as per serving. Cooking tips have also been included at the end of some of the recipes, while the colourful illustrations provide a preview of some of the finished dishes. The chapters at the beginning of the second part of the book provide origin and preparation guidance for some of the foods and flavours used. An index of dishes, is also included before each section to help in finding the relevant recipe quickly. For those who are interested in more specific nutrient content, a special Recipe Composition Table, containing all nutrient information of the items, has been compiled.

It is hoped that *An Adventure in Caribbean Cuisine* will serve not only as a recipe book but also as an educational vehicle that will enable you to journey through and savour both the romance of traditional Caribbean cuisine and the excitement of the contemporary experiments presented here.

Acknowledgements

Caribbean Food and Nutrition Institute (CFNI) for all Nutrition Analyses.
Ms Norma Washington, Principal, Carnegie School of Home Economics, Guyana, for her kind permission to use the recipe for katahar curry.
Gernot Katzner for permission to use information on spices and herbs from his website.
Ninian Blair and Yvette De Freitas, who proved to be very good technical advisers for the organization of the book.
Dr Theodora Alexander and Magda Pollard for reviewing, proofreading and providing invaluable insight.

Thank you everyone.

Janice Archibald
CAHE President (2001–5)

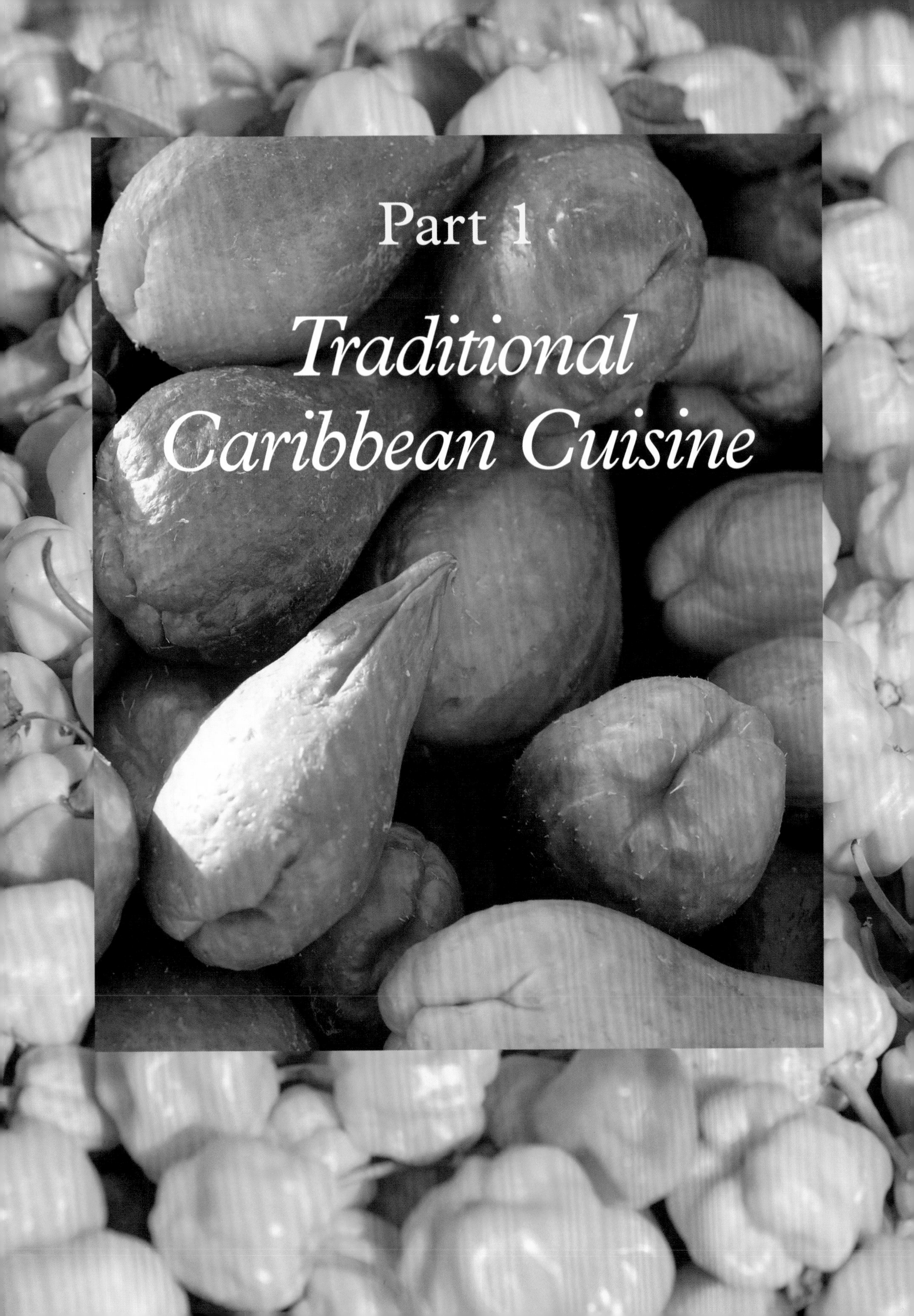

Part 1

Traditional Caribbean Cuisine

Caribbean cuisine in symphony

Imagine … listening to the sweet tones of steelpan music:
sipping coffee flavoured with rich thick coconut milk;
savouring a compote of brightly coloured fruits cut up, sprinkled with demerara sugar and nutmeg, then spiked with a splash of black rum and 'bitters';
relishing thick slices of jerk pork or a plate of stuffed jacks, 'washed down' by a long cold draught of passion-fruit juice or cool fresh coconut water …

'Aaaaaaaaah'

Thoughts of the 'Caribbean' conjure up a mélange of bright colours, vibrant sounds, rich scents, and spicy flavours which permeate the people's behaviour as well as the foods. Over centuries, the cultures have blended while still maintaining some individual characteristics. This process has served to give Caribbean cuisine a more regional identity rather than remaining isolated within the specific territories. Despite this, each territory still maintains its own cultural foods, although the selections have increased due to the increasing availability of other foods. This section seeks to address just a few of the influences on Caribbean cuisine.

Traditionally, this cuisine has evolved as heritage from the many nations that have travelled to the islands and South America, some as conquerors, others as conquered, indentured and settlers. Each nation – Spanish, British, French, Dutch, African, Indian, Portuguese, Chinese, and others – brought cultural food choices and eating patterns which they then sometimes adapted to suit the environment in which they found themselves.

The unusual combination of spices, fruits and vegetables intermingling with a variety of meats has come to be considered traditionally Caribbean or 'Creole', an indication of being quite 'mixed-up', deriving from mixed ethnicity. Some of these foods are used across several of the territories but are known by different names. A fitting example of this is seen with conkie, blue drawers, paimie, pastelles – which are all cornmeal based, sweet or savoury, flavoured and steamed in banana leaves. In other cases foods of the same name are found to be completely different in appearance as well as methods of preparation.

Jerking is a traditional style of cooking that became a speciality in Jamaica and it is not unusual in popular areas to find jerk pits tempting you to stop and sample the fare of jerk pork or other meats, accompanied by roasted breadfruit or yam. It is suggested that the cooking style was developed by the runaway slaves, who killed wild hogs and other animals and learnt to preserve them by rubbing them with pimento berries and smoking the meat over the pimento wood. The term 'jerk' is thought to refer to the process of turning the meat while it is cooking over the pimento wood fires.

The Amerindian or native Indian cultures provided the art of barbecue cooking. They used to cook their hunted game on wooden slats over an open fire, which exposed it to the smoke. The rack was called a 'barbacoa'. They also used a lot of root vegetables, including cassava, which was a source of both food and drink. The juice of the cassava (casareep) was used to cook the meats in what became the famous pepperpot of Guyana and Suriname. Nothing else was added to the meat besides the pepper and casareep – the unusual flavour was totally derived from the casareep. Yet, while the pepperpot of Guyana is a very dark brown, that of Suriname is much lighter in colour.

The name 'pepperpot', however, is also used to describe a thick callaloo soup or a mixed vegetable stew, which in most islands is called simply callaloo. Pepperpot soup, on the other hand, is thought to have originated among Africans who as slaves prepared a communal pot, 'pooled' all their foodstuff and made a one-pot meal from which everyone ate. The combination of a variety of meats, ground provisions and vegetables varies throughout the Caribbean region from a simple Jamaican pepperpot soup (callaloo), which is primarily meat and spinach boiled in seasoned water, to the Jamaican pepperpot, which is a more elaborate version and has included eggplant, ochroes, pumpkin, kale and yams, together with milk and butter, and not forgetting a hot pepper. This is a much thicker soup and is very often accompanied by small dumplings. The Antiguan version also adds green papaw, cloves, garlic, ketchup or tomato paste as well as fresh green peas. This is more like a thick stew than a soup and is served with fungee, a local cornmeal dish.

Variations of pepperpot are served throughout the Caribbean as callaloo, which in Dominica contains crab meat, in Martinique crabs and smoked ham. In Trinidad, crab meat and a hot pepper are added with pumpkin and coconut milk; in the US Virgin Islands, pickled pork ribs and tail plus mashed salmon are included; and in Barbados all ingredients are cooked until soft, then swizzled or stirred vigorously to make a smooth thick mixture to which butter is added. This may be served with foo foo.

Other African influences include the use of highly seasoned foods, which developed from the need to add some flavour to the insipid leftovers which were received from their 'masters' on the plantations. This led to a cooking culture which involved heavy seasonings or marinades in the cooking of all meats. The seasonings often favour a blend of herbs enhanced by ginger, cloves, nutmeg or allspice, each providing its unique flavour or scent. The Africans are also credited with introducing ochro, pigeon peas and callaloo; the Spaniards brought eggplant, garbanzo beans, onions and garlic; curries and oriental spices came from India and China; while black-eye peas and a variety of other peas and beans were eventually introduced from the southern states of America. Most bean dishes are served with rice and cornbread, similar to Creole menus of the southern United States. However, in many Caribbean islands the popular 'peas an' rice' is a must, regardless of the type of peas. This is so even in Guyana, where it is more usual to cook 'white' rice, meaning that nothing is added to the rice during the cooking.

Intermarriage between African slaves and native Caribs from the island of Belize produced the black Caribs, called Garifuna. Traditional Garifuna foods are based on coconut milk, garlic, basil and black pepper. Green banana and plantain are grated, mashed, boiled or baked. Fish boiled in coconut milk, called 'serre', served with mashed plantain, called 'hudut', is a deliciously rich meal.

The warm waters of the Caribbean Sea yield numerous varieties of seafood – snapper, trout, butterfish, dolphin, kingfish, shrimp, lobster, crabs and conch – which can be prepared in a variety of exciting ways, simmered in coconut cream as well as other flavourings, and enhanced with delicious spicy tomato sauces. In addition, dried or preserved seafoods can be served when fresh ones are unavailable. Salted fish is a delicacy in its own right and can give a unique flavour to very simple dishes.

A number of snack items that are truly Caribbean include fritters, basically a batter with any of a range of flavourings – peas, vegetables and meats. These fritters have several names, such as accra, baigani, cala, pulourie, puffs and 'stamp and go'. Then there are chips of plantain, banana, yam, breadfruit and cassava. 'Puddin' an' souse' can be found in many islands. The pudding, known as 'black pudding' in Guyana and some of the territories, is a blood sausage which may have rice, bread, biscuits or potatoes added to make a more substantial filling. More recently, some people, for health and religious reasons, have adapted the delicacy to become 'white pudding' by omitting the blood. Souse is any meat cooked and served in a hot pepper and lime-flavoured pickling liquid. This is generally a weekend favourite in Guyana, Trinidad and Tobago, and Barbados.

The blend of romance and imagination that has moulded the exotic Caribbean cuisine has always been exhilarating. A closer look at some of the dishes in this section will attest to the great initiative, born out of necessity, which has resulted in interesting combinations of foods and flavours and ultimately a variety of dishes which are truly the epitome of traditional Caribbean.

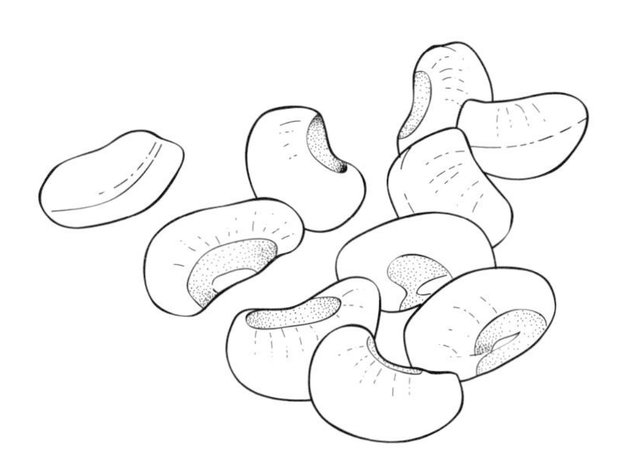

Traditional dishes

Anguilla
Baked eel

Antigua and Barbuda
Antigua Sunday morning breakfast
Antigua pepperpot
Cornmeal – Fungee

Bahamas
Conch chowder
Chicken souse
Johnny cake
Guava duff
Hard sauce

Barbados
Flying fish melts in cheese sauce
'Doved' peas
Cou cou
Jug-jug
Conkies

Belize
Arroz con pollo
Letu banana mulsa

Cayman Islands
Zuppa di pesce
Beer-batter fish
Coconut cream pie
Banana mudslide

Dominica
Crapaud soup
Boogo (wilks) stew
Rabbit 'run-down'
Plantain custard
Tittiri accra

Grenada
Oil down
Pepperpot
Cinnamon fried banana
Nutmeg ice cream

Guyana
Metagee
Pepperpot
Cook up rice
Gulgulla
Cassava bread
Katahar curry

Jamaica
Rice and peas
Sweet potato pudding
Ackee and salt fish

Montserrat
Montserrat mixed marmalade
Montserrat citrus marmalade

St Croix
Maufe
Cowitch fish
Sweet potato dumb bread
Papaya nut cake
Papaya pie

St Kitts and Nevis
Conch fritters
Escoveitched fish
Stuffed avocado salad
Rikkita beef

St Lucia
Labourer's lunch
Stewed chicken dudon
Cassava pone

St Vincent and the Grenadines
Stuffed jacks
Green banana mince pie
Madungo dumplings

Suriname
Nasi goreng
Peanut soup

Trinidad and Tobago
Bul jol
Sancoche
Trinidad peas and rice
Pastelles

Anguilla

The Valley •

Baked eel

¼ pint (140 ml) olive oil
2 tbsp wine vinegar
2 bay leaves plus more for skewering
1 tsp salt
½ tsp pepper
1 tbsp breadcrumbs
2 lb (908 g) eel (large variety), skinned and cut into 4-inch (10-cm) pieces

1. Mix together the oil, vinegar, 2 bay leaves, salt, pepper and breadcrumbs.
2. Marinate the eel pieces in this mixture for about 3 hours, turning frequently.
3. Place the eel pieces on skewers, alternating with bay leaves.
4. Place the skewers in a greased baking dish and bake in a moderate oven, 375°F, for 30 minutes, turning often and brushing with the remaining marinade while cooking.

Serves: 4

Nutrition information

	Per recipe	*Per serving*
Kilocalories	2657.6 kcal	664.4 kcal
Protein	168.52 g	42.13 g
Carbohydrate	5.924 g	1.481 g
Fat	214.16 g	53.54 g
Cholesterol	1142 mg	285.5 mg
Dietary fibre	0.464 g	0.116 g
Sodium	2651.2 mg	662.8 mg
Iron	5.856 mg	1.464 mg

Antigua and Barbuda

St John's
ANTIGUA
BARBUDA

Antigua Sunday morning breakfast

1 lb (454 g) salt fish, soaked, boiled and boned
2 hard-boiled eggs, sliced
1 lb (454 g) antrobers (eggplant), cooked and chopped

For the sauce:
3 tomatoes (Creole)
1 onion, sliced
2 tbsp tomato paste
2 tbsp vegetable oil
salt and pepper
½ tsp chopped garlic
2 tbsp margarine
a little hot sauce

1. Fry all the above sauce ingredients together.
2. Add ¼ pint (140 ml) water and simmer for a few minutes.
3. Arrange the salt fish and antrobers on a platter and decorate with the egg slices.
4. Pour the sauce over the salt fish and antrobers.

Serves: 4

Serve with lettuce, tomato and cucumber slices.

Nutrition information

	Per recipe	*Per serving*
Kilocalories	2160 kcal	540 kcal
Protein	307.4 g	76.85 g
Carbohydrate	57.4 g	14.35 g
Fat	73.9 g	18.47 g
Cholesterol	1114 mg	278.5 mg
Dietary fibre	19.31 g	4.83 g
Sodium	32933 mg	8233.25 mg
Iron	16.33 mg	4.08 mg

Eggplants

Ochroes

Antigua pepperpot

1 lb (454 g) spinach
2 green (fresh) eddo leaves
8 oz (227 g) pumpkin
1 lb (454 g) green papaws
3 table squashes
1 lb (454 g) antrobers (eggplant)
1 lb (454 g) ochroes
1 lb (454 g) salted beef
1 lb (454 g) pig snout
oil for frying
2 onions, sliced
any leftover meats, chopped, or meat skins and bones
12 oz (340 g) fresh green peas
4 cloves
a small piece of garlic
4 tbsp ketchup or tomato paste
chive
thyme

1. Wash all the leaves and vegetables in salted water.
2. Peel the pumpkin, papaw and table squash and cut in pieces; cut up the antrobers and leaves with a sharp knife.
3. Soak and wash the salted meat and snout and cut into neat pieces.
4. Cook the meats in water without adding salt.
5. Remove, drain and fry with the onions.
6. Add the leftover meats and all the vegetables except the peas and stir well.
7. Add just enough water to cover, and cook the vegetables until tender. When the vegetables and meat are cooked, add the peas and season to taste with cloves, garlic, ketchup, chive and thyme.
8. Allow to simmer until thick.

Serves: 4

Serve with ochro fungee rolled in butter or margarine.

Nutrition information

	Per recipe	*Per serving*
Kilocalories	3833 kcal	958.25 kcal
Protein	306 g	76.5 g
Carbohydrate	275.2 g	68.8 g
Fat	179.3 g	44.82 g
Cholesterol	491.4 mg	122.85 mg
Dietary fibre	46.22 g	11.55 g
Sodium	3151 mg	787.75 mg
Iron	75.18 mg	18.79 mg

Cornmeal – Fungee

6 ochroes, cut in pieces
salt to taste
12 oz (340 g) cornmeal

1. Place the ochroes and salt in a pan with 2 pints (1.1 litres) water.
2. Bring to the boil and simmer until the ochroes are cooked.
3. Remove half the liquid and add the remaining liquid and the ochroes in small portions to the cornmeal.
4. Gradually add the removed liquid to the cornmeal mixture.
5. Place the cornmeal mixture in the pan, turning and pressing it against the side of the pan.
6. Cook until there is no taste of flour and the mixture leaves the side of the pan.

Serves: 4

Serve hot with pepperpot, boiled fish or stew.

Nutrition information

	Per recipe	***Per serving***
Kilocalories	1019 kcal	254.7 kcal
Protein	23.97 g	5.99 g
Carbohydrate	216.2 g	54.05 g
Fat	4.162 g	1.04 g
Cholesterol	0 mg	0 mg
Dietary fibre	15.12 g	3.78 g
Sodium	542.8 mg	135.7 mg
Iron	11.54 mg	2.88 mg

Bahamas

GRAND BAHAMA ISLAND
GREAT ABACO ISLAND
ANDROS ISLAND
Nassau
NEW PROVIDENCE ISLAND
SOUTH ANDROS ISLAND

Conch chowder

4 conchs
1 onion
2 celery stalks
1 sweet pepper
2 carrots
1 large potato
3 strips bacon

½ tbsp oil
3 bay leaves
1 tomato, chopped
1 pint (560 ml) tomato juice
1 tsp thyme
salt and black pepper
Worcestershire sauce

1. Grind the conch, onion, celery, sweet pepper and carrots.
2. Dice the potato and chop the bacon.
3. Fry the bacon and add the ground ingredients, potato, bay leaves and tomato.
4. Cover and allow to simmer down over a low heat for 15 minutes. Check occasionally and stir.
5. Add the tomato juice.
6. Season with thyme, salt, black pepper and Worcestershire sauce to taste.
7. Simmer for 1 hour or until the conch is tender.

Serves: 6

Nutrition information

	Per recipe	*Per serving*
Kilocalories	574.38 kcal	95.73 kcal
Protein	34.77 g	5.795 g
Carbohydrate	81.36 g	13.56 g
Fat	15.43 g	2.572 g
Cholesterol	115.98 mg	19.33 mg
Dietary fibre	13.638 g	2.273 g
Sodium	2879.4 mg	479.9 mg
Iron	17.952 mg	2.992 mg

Chicken souse

3 lb (1.8 kg) chicken
2 fresh hot peppers
2 tsp salt
2 tbsp lime juice
1 onion
½ sweet pepper
8 oz (227 g) Irish potatoes

1. Clean the chicken and cut into small pieces.
2. Grind or crush the hot peppers and mix with the salt. Use this to season the chicken.
3. Squeeze the lime juice on the chicken and let stand to marinate for 1 hour (or overnight).
4. Chop the vegetables
5. Place the marinated chicken and the vegetables in a saucepan. Add sufficient water to cover the chicken.
6. Boil for 30 minutes, or until the chicken is tender.
7. Serve in a dish with the gravy as a dip.

Serves: 10

Serve with Johnny cake.

Nutrition information

	Per recipe	***Per serving***
Kilocalories	3156 kcal	315.6 kcal
Protein	339.1 g	33.91 g
Carbohydrate	50.12 g	5.01 g
Fat	168.7 g	16.87 g
Cholesterol	1315 mg	131.5 mg
Dietary fibre	4.754 g	0.47 g
Sodium	5175 mg	517.5 mg
Iron	22.93 mg	2.293 mg

OPPOSITE: *Hot peppers*

Johnny cake

8 oz (227 g) flour
1 tsp salt
3 tsp baking powder
3 tbsp sugar
4 oz (113 g) butter or shortening

1. Mix together the flour, salt, baking powder and sugar in a bowl.
2. Rub in the butter or shortening.
3. Add sufficient water to the flour mixture to make a stiff dough.
4. Knead the dough lightly until smooth.
5. Spread the dough to fit tightly inside a greased 8-inch (20-cm) square baking pan. Prick with a fork.
6. Bake at 350°F for about 35–40 minutes until golden brown.

Serves: 6

Served best with chicken souse or simply as a breakfast meal.

Nutrition information

	Per recipe	***Per serving***
Kilocalories	1879.8 kcal	313.3 kcal
Protein	26.772 g	4.462 g
Carbohydrate	231.18 g	38.53 g
Fat	94.44 g	15.74 g
Cholesterol	248.52 mg	41.42 mg
Dietary fibre	7.242 g	1.207 g
Sodium	4062.6 mg	677.1 mg
Iron	10.122 mg	1.687 mg

Guava duff

8 oz (227 g) flour
3 tsp baking powder
½ tsp salt
4 oz (113 g) butter or hard margarine
2 oz (56 g) sugar
1½–2 lb (681–908 g) guava meat, sliced thinly (see below)
1 egg, beaten
milk

1. Sieve together the flour, baking powder and salt.
2. Rub the butter into the flour with fingertips or pastry blender until the mixture resembles breadcrumbs.
3. Add the sugar and guava meat. Mix.
4. Add the egg and sufficient milk to make a stiff dough. Knead lightly in bowl.
5. Place the dough into a greased 2-quart (1.9-litre) heatproof dish. Cover with foil and seal with string or a rubber band.
6. Place 2 pints (1.1 litres) water in a large pot and bring to the boil.
7. Place the dish in the boiling water. Cover pot and steam for 1½ hours. Add boiling water as needed.
8. Invert the covered duff onto a serving plate. Slice immediately and serve with hard sauce.

Serves: 6

To prepare guavas: wash and peel, then thinly slice the meat, avoiding the seeds.

Nutrition information

	Per recipe	***Per serving***
Kilocalories	2717.4 kcal	452.9 kcal
Protein	40.92 g	6.823 g
Carbohydrate	303.6 g	50.6 g
Fat	151.8 g	25.3 g
Cholesterol	228.42 mg	38.07 mg
Dietary fibre	34.48 g	5.747 g
Sodium	3746.4 mg	624.4 mg
Iron	12.72 mg	2.124 mg

Hard sauce

1 egg white (optional)
8 oz (227 g) butter
1 lb (454 g) sugar
1 tbsp rum or vanilla flavouring

1. Beat the egg white, if using, and set aside.
2. Cream together the butter and sugar until white, light and fluffy.
3. Fold in the flavouring and egg white.
4. Serve with guava duff.

Serves: 6

Nutrition information

	Per recipe	*Per serving*
Kilocalories	3232 kcal	538.6 kcal
Protein	5.448 g	0.91 g
Carbohydrate	404.9 g	67.48 g
Fat	183.8 g	30.63 g
Cholesterol	496.6 mg	78.26 mg
Dietary fibre	0 g	0 g
Sodium	1935 mg	322.5 mg
Iron	0.613 mg	0.10 mg

Barbados

Bridgetown

Flying fish melts in cheese sauce

1½ lb (681 g) melts
juice of 1 lime
4 tbsp margarine
2 tbsp flour
½ pint (280 ml) milk
2 oz (56 g) cheese, grated
1 tbsp chopped parsley
2 tsp grated onion
salt and pepper
1 oz (28 g) white breadcrumbs

1. Wash the melts. Place them in salted water with the lime juice and set aside for a few minutes.
2. Melt 2 tablespoons of the margarine.
3. Mix the flour to a smooth paste with a little milk, then add all the milk.
4. Combine with the melted margarine and stir constantly over a low heat until the mixture thickens and is quite smooth.
5. Add the grated cheese, parsley, onion, and salt and pepper to taste, stirring until the cheese has melted.
6. Drain the melts, and steam them for 5 minutes.
7. Add the melts to the cheese sauce. Pour the mixture into greased individual ramekin dishes, top with white breadcrumbs mixed with 2 tablespoons of melted margarine and bake in a moderate oven, 350°F, until lightly browned.

Serves: 4

Flying fish melts are the soft roe of the fish and are extremely tender and tasty. Serve this dish as an appetizer.

Nutrition information

	Per recipe	*Per serving*
Kilocalories	1638 kcal	409.5 kcal
Protein	116.3 g	29.07 g
Carbohydrate	62.66 g	15.66 g
Fat	100.7 g	25.1 g
Cholesterol	95.39 mg	23.84 mg
Dietary fibre	2.967 g	0.74 g
Sodium	1903 mg	475.7 mg
Iron	8.139 mg	2.03 mg

'Doved' peas

1 lb (454 g) pigeon peas
1 onion, chopped
1 sprig of thyme
4 oz (113 g) ham slices or bacon rashers, chopped
1 red pepper, minced
1 sprig of marjoram
shortening for frying

1. Wash the peas and boil in salted water.
2. Add half the onion and the sprig of thyme.
3. When tender, drain well.
4. Add the chopped ham or bacon, the pepper, remaining onion and marjoram. Mix well with the peas.
5. Fry the mixture in hot shortening until dry.

Serves: 4

Nutrition information

	Per recipe	*Per serving*
Kilocalories	1968 kcal	492 kcal
Protein	115 g	28.7 g
Carbohydrate	264.3 g	66.07 g
Fat	53.76 g	13.44 g
Cholesterol	65.65 mg	16.66 mg
Dietary fibre	1.568 g	0.392 g
Sodium	1700 mg	425 mg
Iron	23.32 mg	5.83 mg

Cou cou

This dish is a savoury cornmeal pudding with ochroes, similar to fungee. It is an old Barbadian favourite served with steamed fish or beef and pork stew. Its origin is the ancient North African couscous, a steamed mixture using different kinds of grain flours with added vegetables and meat.

12 ochroes
3 pints (1.7 litres) water
2 tsp salt
12 oz (340 g) cornmeal
2 tsp cooking butter

1. Wash the ochroes, cut off the stems and slice in rings.
2. Boil in a saucepan with half the water and salt for about 10 minutes.
3. Add the rest of the water and salt to the sifted cornmeal in a bowl and mix well.
4. Remove the saucepan from the heat and blend in the cornmeal mixture.
5. Return the pan to the heat and cook over a medium heat, stirring briskly with a wooden spatula.
6. When the mixture becomes stiff and smooth, cover and allow to steam for a few minutes.
7. When the cou cou breaks away cleanly from the bottom of the saucepan it is ready.
8. Empty into a buttered dish, smooth, and spread liberally with butter. Serve hot.

Serves: 4

Nutrition information

	Per recipe	**Per serving**
Kilocalories	1097 kcal	274.2 kcal
Protein	24.61 g	6.13 g
Carbohydrate	218.4 g	54.6 g
Fat	12.33 g	3.08 g
Cholesterol	20.71 mg	5.17 mg
Dietary fibre	15.87 g	3.97 g
Sodium	4353 mg	1088.2 mg
Iron	11.69 mg	2.92 mg

Jug-jug

2 lb (908 g) corned pork
2 lb (908 g) boneless salted beef
8 pints (4.48 litres) pigeon peas
8 oz (227 g) onions, chopped
8 oz (227 g) green seasoning
thyme
parsley
pepper
12 oz (340 g) Guinea cornflour
2 tbsp margarine

1. Soak the corned pork and salted beef overnight. Pour off the water.
2. Boil together the peas, onions, green seasoning and thyme to taste.
3. Boil the corned pork and salted beef together. When cooked, cut into pieces, reserving the cooking water.
4. Combine the meat with the peas and season with parsley and pepper. Put through the mincer. The mixture should be quite smooth with no peas to be seen.
5. Return to the heat, add the Guinea cornflour and as much of the reserved water as necessary to bring the mixture to a thick dropping consistency.
6. Stir constantly until the cornflour is cooked (about 30 minutes).
7. Add the margarine and continue stirring until smooth.

Serves: 32

Guinea corn is a type of maize or Indian corn.

Nutrition information

	Per recipe	*Per serving*
Kilocalories	20524 kcal	641.37 kcal
Protein	984.6 g	30.76 g
Carbohydrate	2186 g	68.31 g
Fat	898.7 g	28.05 g
Cholesterol	0 mg	0 mg
Dietary fibre	519.6 g	16.23 g
Sodium	844.3 mg	26.38 mg
Iron	255.9 mg	7.99 mg

Coconuts

Pumpkins

Conkies

1 coconut
1½ lb (681 g) pumpkin
8 oz (227 g) sweet potato (optional)
4 oz (113 g) heavy sugar (very dark brown sugar)
340 g (12 oz) Indian cornmeal
1 tsp cinnamon
2 tsp nutmeg
2 tsp shortening
2 tsp margarine
¼ pint (140 ml) milk
2 eggs, beaten
1 tsp almond essence
3 oz (85 g) raisins
salt
plantain leaves

1. Grate the coconut and pumpkin (and sweet potato, if desired).
2. Add the sugar, cornmeal, cinnamon and nutmeg.
3. Melt the shortening and margarine, combine with the milk, and add to the cornmeal mixture.
4. Add the beaten eggs, almond essence, raisins and salt to taste.
5. Cut plantain leaves into 8-inch (20-cm) squares and steam until pliable.
6. Place a few tablespoons of mixture in each plantain leaf square, fold up carefully and tie securely.
7. Steam the conkies on a rack in a large pot or steamer over boiling water until they are firm and cooked (about 1 hour), making sure that no water gets into the conkies.

Serves: 12

The addition of grated sweet potato makes a firmer conkie.

Nutrition information

	Per recipe	*Per serving*
Kilocalories	2838 kcal	236.5 kcal
Protein	55.31 g	4.60 g
Carbohydrate	532 g	44.33 g
Fat	61.16 g	5.11 g
Cholesterol	442.5 mg	36.87 mg
Dietary fibre	38.86 g	3.23 g
Sodium	1094 mg	91.16 mg
Iron	17.37 mg	1.44 mg

Belize

Belmopan

Arroz con pollo

This is a one-pot dinner.

3 tsp fat
1 onion, chopped
1 lb (454 g) chicken, cut into pieces
4 tomatoes, chopped
½ pint (280 ml) water or stock
1 lb (454 g) carrots, sliced and cooked
6 oz (168 g) fresh green peas
1 small sweet pepper, chopped
8 oz (227 g) rice
3 tbsp margarine
¾ tsp salt
⅛ tsp black pepper
2 oz (56 g) grated cheese

1. Heat the fat in a saucepan and fry the onions. Remove from pan.
2. Place the chicken in the pan and fry until brown.
3. Add the onions, tomatoes, water or stock, carrots, green peas and sweet pepper to the chicken. Cook for 5 minutes.
4. Add the rice, margarine, salt and black pepper to the chicken and stir.
5. Reduce the heat and allow the rice to simmer until tender.
6. Add the cheese and simmer until melted.

Serves: 6

Nutrition information

	Per recipe	*Per serving*
Kilocalories	3036.64 kcal	506.10 kcal
Protein	137.77 g	22.96 g
Carbohydrate	299.56 g	49.92 g
Fat	141.63 g	23.60 g
Cholesterol	467.4 mg	77.9 mg
Dietary fibre	16.77 g	2.79 g
Sodium	2965.15 mg	494.19 mg
Iron	28.72 mg	4.78 mg

Bananas

Letu banana mulsa

6 ripe bananas
1 pint (560 ml) coconut milk
a pinch of salt
a pinch of ground ginger
¼ tsp vanilla essence

1. Slice the bananas and boil in ½ pint (280 ml) water until tender.
2. Pour in the coconut milk and add the salt, ginger and essence.
3. Stir gradually until thoroughly blended.
4. Serve hot.

Serves: 4

Nutrition information

	Per recipe	*Per serving*
Kilocalories	868.95 kcal	217.24 kcal
Protein	11.69 g	2.92 g
Carbohydrate	215.84 g	53.96 g
Fat	5.15 g	1.29 g
Cholesterol	0 mg	0 mg
Dietary fibre	11.91 g	2.98 g
Sodium	872.83 mg	218.21mg
Iron	3.91 mg	0.98 mg

Cayman Islands

Zuppa di pesce

1 tbsp oil
4 oz (113 g) snapper
4 oz (113 g) lobster tail
1 jumbo shrimp
8 small shrimps
6 sea scallops
1 oz (28 g) oregano
½ oz (14 g) parsley
½ oz (14 g) basil
2 oz (56 g) diced plum tomato
a pinch of cayenne pepper
¼ pint (140 ml) fish stock

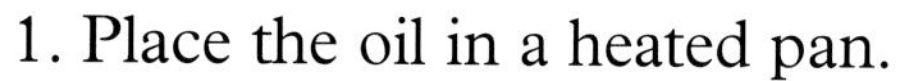

1. Place the oil in a heated pan.
2. Add the snapper, lobster tail, shrimps and scallops and sauté for about 2 minutes.
3. Stir in the fresh herbs, tomato and cayenne pepper.
4. Add the fish stock and leave to cook for about 5 minutes.

Serves: 4

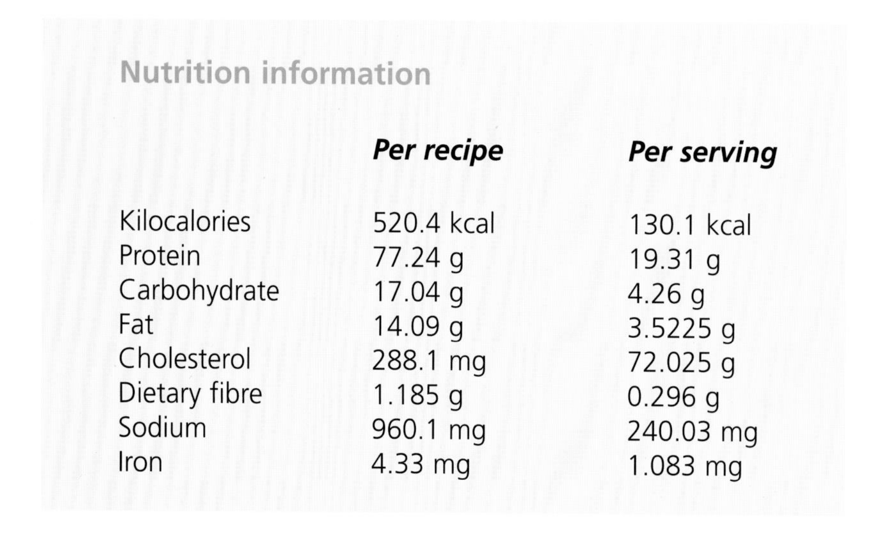

Nutrition information

	Per recipe	*Per serving*
Kilocalories	520.4 kcal	130.1 kcal
Protein	77.24 g	19.31 g
Carbohydrate	17.04 g	4.26 g
Fat	14.09 g	3.5225 g
Cholesterol	288.1 mg	72.025 g
Dietary fibre	1.185 g	0.296 g
Sodium	960.1 mg	240.03 mg
Iron	4.33 mg	1.083 mg

Beer-batter fish

1 pint (560 ml) vegetable oil
2 lb (908 g) fresh fish fillets (snapper or grouper)
1 tbsp fresh lime juice
4 oz (113 g) flour
1 tsp seasoned salt
¼ tsp pepper
1 can beer

1. Fill a deep fryer or a deep saucepan three-quarters full with oil. Heat to 375°F.
2. Cut the fish fillets into serving-size pieces and brush with lime juice.
3. Mix two thirds of the flour with the salt and pepper in a bowl.
4. Add the beer gradually, beating until the batter is smooth.
5. Put the remaining flour on a plate.
6. Coat each piece of fish with flour, then dip it into the batter, coating well.
7. Fry in the hot oil for 7–8 minutes, turning once.
8. Drain on paper towel or brown paper.

Serves: 4

Serve hot with fried potatoes and coleslaw.

Nutrition information

	Per recipe	*Per serving*
Kilocalories	2222.4 kcal	555.6 kcal
Protein	186.24 g	46.56 g
Carbohydrate	112.24 g	28.06 g
Fat	94 g	23.5 g
Cholesterol	0 mg	0 mg
Dietary fibre	5.044 g	1.261 g
Sodium	1541.2 mg	385.3 mg
Iron	14.92 mg	3.729 mg

Coconut cream pie

5 oz (140 g) sugar
5 tbsp cornstarch
½ tsp salt
1½ pints (840 ml) milk
3 egg yolks, lightly beaten
1 tbsp butter
1½ tsp vanilla essence
2 tbsp coconut rum
8 oz (227 g) fresh shredded coconut
baked pie shell
whipped cream for decoration
2 tbsp toasted coconut

1. Place the sugar, cornstarch, salt and milk in a saucepan.
2. Cook over a medium heat, stirring constantly until the mixture thickens.
3. Stir half of the hot mixture into the egg yolks. Return to the saucepan and blend.
4. Boil for 1 minute, stirring constantly.
5. Remove from the heat, and add the butter, vanilla, coconut rum and shredded coconut.
6. Pour into the baked pie shell and chill.
7. Top with whipped cream and sprinkle with toasted coconut.

Serves: 8

Prevent heated milk from scorching by rinsing the pan with hot water before using it.

Nutrition information

	Per recipe	***Per serving***
Kilocalories	3425 kcal	428.12 kcal
Protein	51.84 g	6.48 g
Carbohydrate	311.7 g	38.96g
Fat	216.2 g	27.02 g
Cholesterol	1034 mg	129.25 mg
Dietary fibre	12.79 g	1.598 g
Sodium	2797 mg	349.62 mg
Iron	7.79 mg	0.973 mg

Banana mudslide

Slide into paradise. This is the island's favourite – voted best in the Cayman Islands!

1¼ fl oz (38 ml) vodka
1 fl oz (30 ml) Kahlua
2 fl oz (60 ml) Irish Cream
1 banana, sliced
crushed ice

1. Place all the ingredients except the ice in a blender.
2. Add a scoop of crushed ice and blend until smooth.
3. Serve with a straw in a hurricane glass.

Serves: 1

Nutrition information

	Per recipe	*Per serving*
Kilocalories	428.8 kcal	428.8 kcal
Protein	3.51 g	3.51 g
Carbohydrate	50.36 g	50.36 g
Fat	5.18 g	5.18 g
Cholesterol	34.52 mg	34.52 mg
Dietary fibre	1.94 g	1.94 g
Sodium	35.36 mg	35.36 mg
Iron	0.57 mg	0.57 mg

Dominica

Roseau

Crapaud soup

- 2 crapauds
- salt and white pepper
- 4 carrots
- 1 turnip
- 3–4 potatoes
- 1 leek
- 1 sprig of celery
- 1 small onion, sliced
- 1 garlic clove, crushed
- 5 cloves
- 1 oz (28 g) macaroni
- 2 tbsp butter

1. Clean and cut up the crapauds, and sprinkle with salt and pepper.
2. Peel and dice the carrots, turnip and potatoes.
3. Put the vegetables to boil in 2 pints (1.1 litres) water.
4. Add the leek and celery and boil for 20 minutes.
5. Add the crapauds, onion, garlic, cloves and macaroni.
6. Allow the soup to simmer for another 20 minutes.
7. Add butter, salt and pepper to taste.
8. If the soup is to be used as a first course, strain and serve. If it is to be used as a main dish, serve with the vegetables.

Serves: 4

Nutrition information

	Per recipe	*Per serving*
Kilocalories	1172.8 kcal	293.2 kcal
Protein	92.88 g	23.22 g
Carbohydrate	144.16 g	36.04 g
Fat	26.036 g	6.51 g
Cholesterol	288.2 mg	72.05 mg
Dietary fibre	19.816 g	4.954 g
Sodium	1216.4 mg	304.1 mg
Iron	14.39 mg	3.6 mg

Boogo (wilks) stew

The wilks is a seafood, in a very hard shell. Collect them from the rocks nearest to the sea, or on the sea bed. Boil the wilks for a long time so that the flesh can be easily extracted. Wash and clean the extracted wilks before using.

1 lb (454 g) boiled wilks
4 tbsp peanut or corn oil
4 oz (113 g) onion, finely chopped
½ oz (14 g) garlic
2 oz (56 g) curry powder
3 drops of browning
2 oz (56 g) butter
1 chicken bouillon cube
1 tbsp lime juice
salt

1. Mince the wilks.
2. Heat the oil in a pan and cook the onion and garlic with the curry powder until brown.
3. Add the minced wilks and browning. Stir gently until the wilks turn brown. Add the butter, crumble the bouillon cube into the stew and add the lime juice and salt to taste.
4. Cook the wilks until tender, adding a little water to the stew.

Serves: 4

Nutrition information

	Per recipe	***Per serving***
Kilocalories	6701 kcal	1675 kcal
Protein	33.58 g	8.39 g
Carbohydrate	74.94 g	18.73 g
Fat	715 g	178.7 g
Cholesterol	241.6 mg	60.4 mg
Dietary fibre	21.05 g	5.26 g
Sodium	2350 mg	587.5 mg
Iron	43.6 mg	10.9 mg

Rabbit 'run-down'

2 lb (908 g) rabbit
1 pint (560 ml) coconut milk
1 tbsp salt
1 tbsp curry powder
1 eschallot stalk, finely chopped
1 sprig of thyme
1 small hot pepper, crushed
2 garlic cloves, finely chopped
6 dried pimento (allspice) berries

1. Cut the rabbit into serving portions.
2. Bring the coconut milk to the boil and add the rabbit, salt and curry powder.
3. Cover, reduce the heat and simmer for 1 hour, or until tender.
4. Add all other flavouring ingredients 5 minutes before removing from the heat.

Serves: 6

Nutrition information

	Per recipe	*Per serving*
Kilocalories	2368 kcal	394.66 kcal
Protein	194.3 g	32.38 g
Carbohydrate	33.68 g	5.61 g
Fat	165.8 g	27.63 g
Cholesterol	513.5 mg	85.6 mg
Dietary fibre	4.51 g	0.75 g
Sodium	6843 mg	1140.5 mg
Iron	24.15 mg	4.03 mg

Plantain custard

3 over-ripe plantains
¾ pint (420 ml) evaporated milk
2 eggs
1 oz (28 g) sugar
rind of 1 lime
1 tsp nutmeg

1. Peel and slice the plantains.
2. Lay the plantains in a greased ovenproof dish.
3. Heat the evaporated milk to warm.
4. Break the eggs into a bowl and whisk lightly with the sugar and lime rind.
5. Add the warm milk and continue whisking until the mixture is well blended but not frothy.
6. Pour over the plantains and top with the nutmeg.
7. Bake at 325°F for about 30 minutes until the custard is firm and the plantains are cooked.

Serves: 4

To prevent a skin forming on custard, cover the surface immediately it is cooked with damp greaseproof paper.

Nutrition information

	Per recipe	***Per serving***
Kilocalories	1602 kcal	400.5 kcal
Protein	44.13 g	11.03 g
Carbohydrate	289.7 g	72.42 g
Fat	40.78 g	10.19 g
Cholesterol	535.7 mg	133.92 mg
Dietary fibre	16.55 g	4.13 g
Sodium	564.6 mg	141.15 mg
Iron	6.405 mg	1.60 mg

Tittiri accra

1 lb (454 g) tittiri
2–3 blades of chive, chopped
½ hot pepper, chopped finely
¼ tsp salt
about 8 oz (227 g) flour
1 pint (560 ml) vegetable oil

1. Soak and wash the tittiri thoroughly, being careful to remove straws and stones.
2. Add the chopped chive, pepper, salt and ½ pint (280 ml) water.
3. Using flour as required, mix to form a creamy paste.
4. Heat the oil and drop the mixture by spoonfuls into the hot oil.
5. Fry to a crisp golden colour and serve hot.

Serves: 12

Tittiri accra should be prepared 30 minutes before ready to cook.

Nutrition information

	Per recipe	*Per serving*
Kilocalories	1247 kcal	103.9 kcal
Protein	103.6 g	8.63 g
Carbohydrate	194.3 g	16.19 g
Fat	3.808 g	0.32 g
Cholesterol	0 mg	0 mg
Dietary fibre	7.311 g	0.61 g
Sodium	683.6 mg	56.96 mg
Iron	13.59 mg	1.13 mg

Grenada

St George's

Oil down

8 oz (227 g) salted meat
1 onion, chopped
1 sprig each of celery, chive and thyme
2 seasoning peppers, chopped
1 large breadfruit
2 carrots, chopped
1 lb (454 g) dumplings (see page 42)
1–2 pints (560 ml–1.1 litres) coconut milk
2 tbsp turmeric or saffron
8–10 young dasheen leaves

1. Soak the salted meat overnight.
2. Boil the meat for about 15 minutes in a heavy pot.
3. Add the onion, celery, chive, thyme and seasoning peppers.
4. Peel and slice the breadfruit and arrange on top of the meat. Add the carrots and dumplings, then the coconut milk and turmeric. Place the dasheen leaves at the top.
5. Cover the pot tightly and cook on medium heat until all the liquid is absorbed.
6. Remove the dasheen leaves when cooked and stir slightly.
7. Serve the dasheen leaves along with the breadfruit and meat

Serves: 5

Any other meat may be used instead of salted meat.

Nutrition information

	Per recipe	*Per serving*
Kilocalories	3453 kcal	690.6 kcal
Protein	94.12 g	18.82 g
Carbohydrate	278.3 g	55.66 g
Fat	236.5 g	47.3 g
Cholesterol	14.45 mg	2.89 mg
Dietary fibre	30.52 g	6.10 g
Sodium	2380 mg	476 mg
Iron	36.52 mg	7.30 mg

Pepperpot

1 lb (454 g) shin of beef
8 oz (227 g) beans
5 spinach or dasheen leaves
2 onions
1 lb (454 g) yam or dasheen
8 oz (227 g) pumpkin
1 tomato
1 chilli pepper
1 sprig of thyme
1 garlic clove
1 beef stock cube

For the dumplings:
12 oz (340 g) plain flour
4 oz (113 g) cornmeal
½ tsp salt

1. Wash and cut up the meat.
2. Cover with 3 pints (1.7 litres) water and boil with the beans for 15–20 minutes.
3. Chop the vegetables and add to the pan with the remaining ingredients.
4. Cook for 1 hour.
5. To make the dumplings, mix the flour, cornmeal and salt with a little water.
6. Roll into balls with your hands.
7. Drop into the boiling mixture and cook for the final 15 minutes.

Serves: 5

Pepperpot is delicious heated up the next day.

Nutrition information

	Per recipe	*Per serving*
Kilocalories	3467.5 kcal	693.5 kcal
Protein	146.5 g	29.3 g
Carbohydrate	502 g	100.4 g
Fat	95.45 g	19.09 g
Cholesterol	305.85 mg	61.17 mg
Dietary fibre	28.92 g	5.783 g
Sodium	2249.5 mg	449.9 mg
Iron	44.76 mg	8.951 mg

Cinnamon fried banana

1 large slightly green banana
2 tsp butter
1¾ tbsp brown sugar
¼ tbsp cinnamon

1. Slice the banana lengthwise into equal slices.
2. Fry the slices in a little butter until slightly brown on both sides.
3. Brush the butter thinly over the banana and fry for a further few minutes.
4. Mix the sugar and cinnamon, then sprinkle each slice with the mixture.

Serves: 2

Serve with ice cream or whipped cream.

Nutrition information

	Per recipe	*Per serving*
Kilocalories	267.9 kcal	133.9 kcal
Protein	1.328 g	0.664 g
Carbohydrate	51.49 g	25.75g
Fat	8.269 g	4.13 g
Cholesterol	20.71 mg	10.36 mg
Dietary fibre	1.94 g	0.97 g
Sodium	89.02 mg	44.51 mg
Iron	1.483 mg	0.74 mg

Nutmeg ice cream

¾ pint (420 ml) milk
¾ pint (420 ml) heavy cream
3 large eggs
6 oz (170 g) sugar
1 tbsp freshly grated nutmeg
⅛ tbsp salt
¼ tbsp vanilla essence

1. Place the milk and cream in a saucepan and bring to the boil.
2. Whisk together the eggs, sugar, nutmeg, salt and vanilla essence in a bowl.
3. Add half of the milk mixture to the eggs and continue whisking.
4. Stir in the remainder of the milk mixture and return to the heat.
5. Cook the custard over moderate heat, stirring constantly with a wooden spoon until it registers 175°F (79°C) on a candy thermometer.
6. Transfer the custard to a metal bowl set in a large bowl of ice and cold water. Stir until it is cold.
7. Freeze the custard in an ice-cream freezer according to the manufacturer's instructions.

Makes: 1 quart (1.1 litres)
Serves: 8

Nutrition information

	Per recipe	***Per serving***
Kilocalories	2276 kcal	284.5 kcal
Protein	38.25 g	4.78 g
Carbohydrate	180.4 g	22.55 g
Fat	160.2 g	20.02 g
Cholesterol	1177 mg	147.15 mg
Dietary fibre	0 g	0 g
Sodium	772.4 mg	96.55 mg
Iron	2.607 mg	0.32 mg

Guyana

Georgetown

Metagee

8 oz (227 g) eddoes (tannia)
8 oz (227 g) cassava
8 oz (227 g) green plantains
8 oz (227 g) firm ripe plantains
8 oz (227 g) yams
1 coconut, grated
1 onion, diced
1 blade of celery, chopped
2 blades of eschallot, chopped
8 oz (227 g) flour
½ tbsp margarine
2 tsp baking powder
2 tbsp sugar
1½ lb (681 g) pieces of fried fish

1. Peel the ground provisions.
2. Add 2 pints (1.1 litres) water to the coconut, squeeze out and strain the milk.
3. Put the prepared ground provision in a pot and add the coconut milk, onion, celery and eschallot. Cook over a moderate heat until the vegetables are tender and the coconut milk has reduced.
4. Mix the flour with the margarine, baking powder and sugar and add enough water to make a soft dough.
5. Divide the dough into pieces and shape into oblongs. Place on top of the provision about 10 minutes before the end of cooking time.
6. Cover and leave to steam for 8 minutes. Add the fried fish and cook for an additional 2 minutes.

Serves: 10

Boiling the coconut milk for metagee before adding the ground provision results in an oily dish. For less oil, add the vegetables before the milk is boiled.

Nutrition information

	Per recipe	***Per serving***
Kilocalories	3869 kcal	386.9 kcal
Protein	121.4 g	12.14 g
Carbohydrate	630 g	63 g
Fat	107.5 g	10.75 g
Cholesterol	0 mg	0 mg
Dietary fibre	28.93 g	2.89 g
Sodium	1855 mg	185.5 mg
Iron	31.01 mg	3.1 mg

Eddoes

Plantains

Yams

Pepperpot

8 oz (227 g) cow heel (or pig's feet)
8 oz (227 g) stewing steak (or pork)
8 oz (227 g) cow face (goat's head)
8 oz (227 g) ox tail
½ pint (280 ml) casareep
1 hot pepper
2 tbsp sugar
1 tsp salt
6 cloves
1-inch (2.5-cm) piece of cinnamon stick
1-inch (2.5-cm) piece of orange peel

1. Cut the meat into pieces and rinse with cool water.
2. Cook each meat separately until all the liquid has dried out.
3. Put the meats into one pot and add the casareep, 1 pint (560 ml) water, the pepper, sugar, salt, cloves, cinnamon and orange peel.
4. Simmer until tender. Adjust seasoning to taste.

Serves: 4

Ox tail, cow heel and cow face may need to be cooked in a pressure cooker to soften. Pepperpot is best if used 2–3 days after preparation.

Nutrition information

	Per recipe	*Per serving*
Kilocalories	2146 kcal	536.5 kcal
Protein	214.2 g	53.55 g
Carbohydrate	50.28 g	12.57 g
Fat	115.4 g	28.85 g
Cholesterol	2053 mg	513.3 mg
Dietary fibre	4.216 g	1.05 g
Sodium	2642 mg	660.5 mg
Iron	17.63 mg	4.41 mg

Cook up rice

8 oz (227 g) salted beef and/or pig tail
8 oz (227 g) chicken
2 garlic cloves, chopped
½ tsp black pepper
8 oz (227 g) peas (pigeon, black-eye, etc.)
1 coconut, grated
1 lb (454 g) rice
1 onion
2 blades of eschallot
1 celery stalk
4 tbsp ketchup

1. Boil the salted beef or pig tail until most of the salt has been removed.
2. Cut up the chicken and season with the garlic and black pepper.
3. Soak the peas for 1½ hours. Add to the salted meat and boil until tender.
4. Add 2 pints (1.1 litres) water to the grated coconut, squeeze and strain the milk.
5. Add the coconut milk to the cooked peas. Add the chicken and simmer for 5 minutes.
6. Wash the rice, then add to the pot with the onion, eschallot, celery and ketchup.
7. Bring to the boil and adjust flavour to taste.
8. Reduce the heat and simmer for 45 minutes or until the rice is cooked.

Serves: 5

Nutrition information

	Per recipe	*Per serving*
Kilocalories	3439 kcal	687.8 kcal
Protein	193.8 g	38.76 g
Carbohydrate	465.9 g	93.18 g
Fat	87.19 g	17.44 g
Cholesterol	242.8 mg	48.56 mg
Dietary fibre	17.57 g	3.51 g
Sodium	449 mg	89.8 mg
Iron	52.91 mg	10.58 mg

Gulgulla

8 oz (227 g) flour
2 tsp baking powder
1 tbsp margarine
2 oz (56 g) sugar
2 oz (56 g) raisins
¼ tsp mixed spice
¼ tsp nutmeg
1 egg
½ tsp vanilla essence
1 banana
4 tbsp milk
1 pint (560 ml) vegetable oil
icing sugar (optional)

1. Sieve the flour and baking powder together.
2. Rub the margarine into the flour mixture.
3. Add the sugar, raisins, spice and nutmeg to the flour mixture.
4. Beat the egg and essence together and put aside.
5. Crush the banana.
6. Add the egg, banana and milk to the flour mixture. Mix to a soft consistency.
7. Heat the oil.
8. Drop the mixture by teaspoonful, or from between wet fingers, into the hot oil. Fry slowly to a light brown colour.
9. Drain on absorbent paper.
10. If desired, dust lightly with icing sugar before serving.

Serves: 12

Serve as dessert or as a sweetmeat.

Nutrition information

	Per recipe	*Per serving*
Kilocalories	1914 kcal	159.5 kcal
Protein	34.85 g	2.90 g
Carbohydrate	308.2 g	25.68 g
Fat	62.53 g	5.21 g
Cholesterol	221.3 mg	18.44 mg
Dietary fibre	10.89 g	0.90 g
Sodium	916.7 mg	76.39 mg
Iron	11.36 mg	0.94 mg

Cassava bread

3 lb (1.4 kg) cassava
2 tsp salt

1. Peel and thoroughly wash the cassava.
2. Finely grate the cassava, add the salt and mix well. Taking only a cupful of wet meal at a time, wring out all the juice.
3. Crumble the meal between the palms of the hands and pass it through a fine sieve.
4. Put a baking stone on an evenly glowing fire, and sprinkle a little cassava meal on it.
5. When the meal browns, brush away from the stone and put a hoop (about 5 inches/12.5 cm in diameter) in place.
6. Spread about an eighth of the meal evenly in the hoop. After 2–3 minutes remove the hoop and flatten and press the bread into shape, using a wooden palette or large knife.
7. As soon as the bread is firm enough, turn it frequently, then remove from the heat.
8. Place in the sun to dry in order to improve flavour and crispness.

Makes: 8

Nutrition information

	Per recipe	*Per serving*
Kilocalories	657.7 kcal	82.21 kcal
Protein	5.443 g	0.68 g
Carbohydrate	159.2 g	19.9 g
Fat	1.361 g	0.17 g
Cholesterol	0 mg	0 mg
Dietary fibre	0 g	0 g
Sodium	4264 mg	533 mg
Iron	3.175 mg	0.39 mg

Katahar curry

1 large katahar (green breadnut fruit)
2 large onions
½ head garlic
1 large hot pepper
1 tbsp ground garam masala
1 tsp ground gheera
2 tbsp curry powder
2 tbsp salt
1 tbsp vegetable oil
½–1 pint (280–560 ml) coconut milk

1. Wash the katahar and cut into pieces. Peel, and cut out the core. Set katahar meat aside and peel the seeds. Cut seeds into small pieces.
2. Wash the katahar meat and drain. Wash the onions and garlic with the hot pepper, then chop and grind.
3. Make a masala paste with the onion mixture, garam masala, gheera, curry powder and salt.
4. Heat the oil in a large carahee. Add the masala paste and katahar seeds and fry for 3–5 minutes. Add the katahar and fry for 3 minutes.
5. Cover and cook for 2 minutes. Add ½ pint (280 ml) coconut milk and stir. Cook for 20 minutes, adding more coconut milk if it becomes too dry. Test for flavour.
6. Continue to cook until most of the liquid has evaporated.

Serves: 12

Serve hot with rice and dhal.
This dish is traditionally served as one of the seven curries at jandies and weddings.

Nutrition information

	Per recipe	***Per serving***
Kilocalories	4608 kcal	309 kcal
Protein	61.33 g	5.111 g
Carbohydrate	560.4 g	46.7 g
Fat	146.28 g	12.19 g
Cholesterol	0 mg	0 mg
Dietary fibre	104.23 g	3.985 g
Sodium	4590 mg	382.5 mg
Iron	95.34 mg	7.945 mg

Jamaica

Kingston

Rice and peas

(Jamaican coat of arms)

8 oz (227 g) dried red peas (kidney beans)
1 pint (560 ml) coconut milk
1 lb (454 g) brown rice
2 garlic cloves, chopped
1 eschallot stalk, chopped
1 green hot pepper, slit half open
1½ tsp salt
1 sprig of thyme

1. Soak the peas in 1 pint (560 ml) water for 2–4 hours or overnight.
2. Cook in the soaking water with another ½ pint (280 ml) water and the coconut milk in a heavy-duty pot with a tightly fitting lid, for about an hour or until tender.
3. Add the rice and all the seasoning ingredients.
4. Stir well, adding ½–1 pint (280–560 ml) more water if necessary. Cover and let simmer for 30 minutes until the rice is tender and the liquid is absorbed.
5. Remove the thyme and pepper before serving.

Serves: 6

Cook the peas with soaked pig's tail or corned pork or beef and omit the salt.
Use 1 lb (454 g) mature peas instead of dried peas.
Add a few dried pimento berries when cooking the peas together with a dab of margarine.

Nutrition information

	Per recipe	*Per serving*
Kilocalories	3906 kcal	651 kcal
Protein	78.96 g	13.16 g
Carbohydrate	407.04 g	67.84 g
Fat	155.2 g	38.8 g
Cholesterol	0 mg	0 mg
Dietary fibre	23.88 g	3.985 g
Sodium	4456.2 mg	742.7 mg
Iron	41.34 mg	6.89 mg

Sweet potatoes

Sweet potato pudding

8 oz (227 g) sweet potato
8 oz (227 g) dasheen, yam or coco (eddoes)
2 oz (56 g) wheat flour
3 oz (84 g) dried fruit
2 oz (56 g) cherries
1–2 tsp freshly grated ginger
2 tsp nutmeg or mixed spice
a dash of black pepper
12 oz (340 g) brown sugar
½ tsp salt
2 pints (1.1 litres) coconut milk
1½ tsp vanilla essence
1½ tsp almond essence or rose water
4 tsp margarine

1. Wash, peel and grate the potato and dasheen, yam or coco. Add the flour, dried fruit, cherries, ginger, nutmeg or mixed spice, and black pepper and mix well.
2. Add the sugar and salt to the coconut milk and stir. Add this to the potato mixture.
3. Add the vanilla and the almond or rose water and stir well.
4. Pour into a 3–4-lb (1.4–1.8-kg) greased round or loaf pan.
5. Dot with the margarine and bake for about 1½ hours at 350°F.
6. Cool, and serve as a snack.

Serves: 12

Alternatively, place ½-pint (140-ml) portions on squares of quailed, pliable green banana leaves, fold securely and steam for 1 hour. (To quail banana leaves, pass them quickly over heat until they become limp and easy to fold.)

Nutrition information

	Per recipe	***Per serving***
Kilocalories	4682.4 kcal	390.2 kcal
Protein	45.48 g	3.79 g
Carbohydrate	614.76 g	51.23 g
Fat	248.28 g	20.69 g
Cholesterol	0 mg	0 mg
Dietary fibre	19.8 g	1.65 g
Sodium	1898.4 mg	158.2 mg
Iron	35.04 mg	2.92 mg

Ackee and salt fish

(National dish of Jamaica)

12 ackee pods
5 oz (140 g) salted fish, soaked for 1–2 hours
1 onion
2 cooking tomatoes
1 eschallot stalk
a small piece of hot pepper
1 sprig of thyme
2 tbsp cooking oil
a sprinkling of black pepper

1. Remove the ackees from pods, discard the seeds and red membranes. Set the yellow arilli (pegs) aside.
2. Clean the prepared ackees in 2 pints (1.1 litres) boiling water.
3. Drain the fish. Remove the bones and flake.
4. Chop the onion, tomatoes and seasoning ingredients. Fry lightly in hot oil for 2 minutes.
5. Add the flaked fish and drained ackee and toss for 1–2 minutes.
6. Remove the thyme and sprinkle the mixture with black pepper.

Serves: 3

Serve hot with roasted breadfruit and avocado pear or with any other starchy food and vegetable of choice.

Nutrition information

	Per recipe	***Per serving***
Kilocalories	773.4 kcal	257.8 kcal
Protein	42.3 g	14.01 g
Carbohydrate	8.91 g	2.973 g
Fat	63.44 g	21.16 g
Cholesterol	82.59 mg	27.53 mg
Dietary fibre	1.72 g	0.575 g
Sodium	711 mg	237 mg
Iron	3.15 mg	1.051 mg

Montserrat

Montserrat mixed marmalade

1 orange
1 lime
1 grapefruit
1 pineapple
about 2 lb (908 g) granulated sugar

1. Wash the citrus fruits and slice finely with a sharp knife, removing the seeds.
2. Peel the pineapple and cut into small pieces.
3. Measure out three times as much water as fruit. Combine and let stand overnight, covered.
4. Uncover and boil briskly for 15 minutes or until the peel is soft. Let stand for 24 hours.
5. Measure out the same volume of sugar as fruit. Boil together until the mixture reaches 221°F (105°C) and jellies, or use saucer test (below).
6. Pour into clean heated glass jars and seal.

Makes: 4 x 8-oz (227-g) jars

To check if marmalade will set use the saucer test. Put a saucer in the freezer to chill. Spoon a little marmalade from the pan onto the chilled saucer. Push carefully with the finger, if the surface wrinkles the marmalade has reached setting point.

Nutrition information

	Per recipe	***Per serving***
Kilocalories	3475 kcal	289.5 kcal
Protein	4.874 g	0.40 g
Carbohydrate	898.6 g	74.88 g
Fat	2.538 g	0.21 g
Cholesterol	0 mg	0 mg
Dietary fibre	14.04 g	1.17 g
Sodium	17.99 mg	1.49 mg
Iron	3.035 mg	0.25 mg

Montserrat citrus marmalade

4 'sibble-sweet' or Seville oranges
1 grapefruit
1 tbsp lime juice
about 3 lb (1.4 kg) granulated sugar

1. Wash the oranges and grapefuit. Place whole, one layer deep in a pan, cover with water, and boil until the skins are soft. Allow to cool in the water overnight. Drain, reserving the liquid.
2. Slice the peel thinly, remove the seeds and any thick white pith from the pulp.
3. Combine the liquid, peel, pulp and lime juice with an equal volume of sugar.
4. If the mixture is very thick, add up to 1 pint (560 ml) extra water.
5. Boil until the marmalade begins to set (see page 59).
6. Bottle in clean, heated glass jars, covering while still hot.

Makes: 4 x 8-oz (227-g) jars

Nutrition information

	Per recipe	*Per serving*
Kilocalories	4962 kcal	413.5 kcal
Protein	6.348 g	0.53 g
Carbohydrate	1281 g	106.75 g
Fat	0.889 g	0.074 g
Cholesterol	0 mg	0 mg
Dietary fibre	16 g	1.33 g
Sodium	18.15 mg	1.51 mg
Iron	1.549 mg	0.13 mg

St Croix

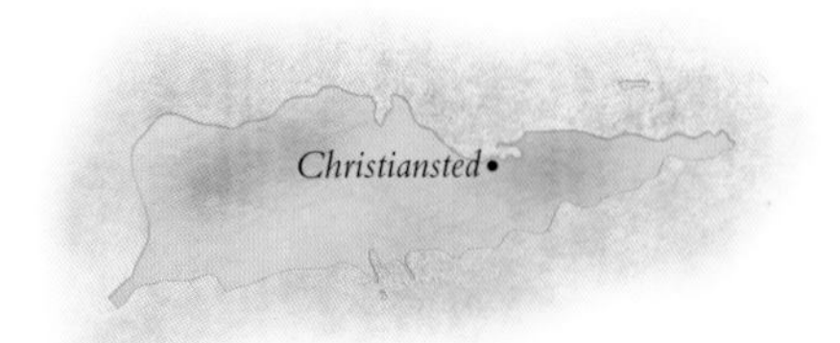

Maufe

1 lb (454 g) pig snout
1 lb (454 g) cooking ham with bone
1 lb (454 g) pork ribs or beef ribs
1 ripe tomato, chopped
2 lb (908 g) fried boned bluefish
2 tsp chopped parsley
2 tsp chopped celery
5 tbsp chopped chives
4 sprigs of fresh thyme, tied in a bundle
1 oz (28 g) cornmeal
1 hot pepper (optional)

1. Cut the meat into serving portions and soak overnight to remove excess salt.
2. Simmer the meat in a large pot until soft. Measure the cooking liquid and add water if necessary, to increase volume to 3 pints (1.7 litres).
3. Add the chopped tomato and cook for 2 minutes.
4. Add the fish and continue to cook for 10 minutes.
5. Add the parsley, celery, chives, thyme and hot pepper, if using, and cook for an additional 10 minutes.
6. Make a paste with the cornmeal and 6 fl oz (210 ml) water and use to thicken the soup mixture to a stew-like consistency.
7. Lower the heat and allow to cook slowly for about 10 minutes or longer, stirring constantly to prevent lumping and sticking. Remove the thyme and hot pepper before serving.

Serves: 8

Serve with plain fungee.
If maufe becomes too thick upon cooling, it can be thinned by adding hot water.

Nutrition information

	Per recipe	***Per serving***
Kilocalories	4900.8 kcal	612.6 kcal
Protein	501.68 g	62.71 g
Carbohydrate	35.08 g	4.385 g
Fat	29.08 g	36.36 g
Cholesterol	1508 mg	188.5 mg
Dietary fibre	3.52 g	0.44 g
Sodium	6185.6 mg	773.2 mg
Iron	22.30 mg	2.788 mg

Cowitch fish

2 lb (908 g) jack fish or king fish slices (6 slices)
2 garlic cloves, crushed
¼ pint (140 ml) oil for frying
½ pint (280 ml) vinegar
¼ pint (140 ml) olive oil
¼ pint (140 ml) corn oil
a few cloves
a few pieces of mace
1 bay leaf
1 small onion, cut in rings

1. Season the fish with salt, pepper and the crushed garlic. Let it stand for at least 30 minutes before frying.
2. Pan fry the fish in hot oil until lightly brown. Drain.
3. Combine all the other ingredients and simmer together gently for a few minutes.
4. Lay the cooked fish in a china or glass container, large enough to hold the fish in no more than two layers.
5. Pour the boiled mixture over the fish and refrigerate until the next day.
6. If the fish is not completely covered by the sauce, turn it to the other side.

Serves: 6

The fish can be served straight from the refrigerator or allowed to stand. Cowitch can last for quite some time. The longer it stands the tastier it becomes, and it is at its best at room temperature.

Nutrition information

	Per recipe	***Per serving***
Kilocalories	3766 kcal	627.8 kcal
Protein	183.5 g	30.59 g
Carbohydrate	18.98 g	3.162 g
Fat	329.6 g	54.94 g
Cholesterol	426.9 mg	71.15 mg
Dietary fibre	1.19 g	0.198 g
Sodium	784.9 mg	130.8 mg
Iron	12.59 mg	2.098 mg

Sweet potato dumb bread

¼ tsp salt
4 oz (113 g) flour
2 tsp baking powder
3 tbsp margarine
12 oz (340 g) sweet potato, grated
about 4 tbsp milk

1. Sift the dry ingredients together and cut in the margarine.
2. Add the grated sweet potato.
3. Add enough milk to make a soft dough.
4. Turn onto a floured board and knead gently.
5. Shape into balls and flatten into biscuit-shaped rounds.
6. Place on a greased baking sheet and bake at 425°F for about 15–20 minutes, until cooked.

Serves: 8

Nutrition information

	Per recipe	*Per serving*
Kilocalories	1023.2 kcal	127.9 kcal
Protein	20.30 g	2.538 g
Carbohydrate	146.08 g	18.26 g
Fat	39.51 g	4.939 g
Cholesterol	16.50 mg	2.063 mg
Dietary fibre	8.91 g	1.114 g
Sodium	1727.2 mg	215.9 mg
Iron	5.82 mg	0.727 mg

Papaya nut cake

4 oz (113 g) shortening
8 oz (227 g) granulated sugar
4 oz (113 g) dark brown sugar
3 eggs
1 tsp vanilla essence
½ tsp almond essence
6 oz (168 g) walnuts, chopped, plus extra for decorating
1 lb (454 g) hard yellow papaya (papaw), grated
1 small soft ripe papaya (papaw), mashed
14 oz (396 g) plain flour
4½ tsp baking powder
⅛ tsp mixed spice
2 tbsp dark molasses
1 tsp baking soda
2 tbsp vegetable oil
1 tsp cinnamon

1. Cream the shortening and sugars until light.
2. Add the eggs, one at a time, beating well after each addition.
3. Add the vanilla and almond essence, nuts and shredded and mashed papaya.
4. Sieve the flour, baking powder and mixed spice together and gradually add to the egg mixture to make a stiff batter.
5. Combine the molasses, baking soda, oil and cinnamon with 1 tablespoon water.
6. Gently fold into the cake batter.
7. Pour into a 9 x 9 x 1¾-inch (22.5 x 22.5 x 4-cm) cake pan.
8. Sprinkle some chopped walnuts over the top.
9. Bake at 350°F for 50 minutes.

Serves: 12

Nutrition information

	Per recipe	*Per serving*
Kilocalories	5124 kcal	427 kcal
Protein	103.32 g	8.61 g
Carbohydrate	661.08 g	55.09 g
Fat	237 g	19.75 g
Cholesterol	639 mg	53.25 mg
Dietary fibre	24.24 g	2.02 g
Sodium	3009.6 mg	250.8 mg
Iron	33.22 mg	2.768 mg

Papaya pie

1 lb (454 g) ripe papayas (papaw)
6 oz (168 g) sugar
2 tsp flour
⅛ tsp salt
¼ tsp nutmeg
⅛ tsp cinnamon
1 tbsp butter

For the pastry:
6 oz (168 g) flour
½ tsp salt
4 oz (113 g) shortening
5 tbsp iced water to mix
1 tsp lemon or lime juice

1. Make the pastry. Sieve together the flour and salt. Add the shortening and rub into the flour until it looks like fine breadcrumbs. Bind with the water and lemon or lime juice.
2. Peel and slice the papayas thinly, in the same way as slicing apples for apple pie.
3. Mix together the sugar, flour, salt and spices.
4. Line a pie plate with the pastry. Fill with the sliced papaya and cover with the sugar mixture.
5. Add 1 tablespoon water and dot with butter.
6. Bake at 400°F for about 50 minutes or until the fruit juice looks clear and thick.
7. Reduce the heat to 350°F to allow the fruit to cook slowly but thoroughly.

Serves: 8

The lime or lemon juice gives a flaky tender crust to the pastry.
This dessert is delicious served with ice cream.

Nutrition information

	Per recipe	*Per serving*
Kilocalories	2499.2 kcal	312.4 kcal
Protein	22.95 g	2.869 g
Carbohydrate	348.88 g	43.61 g
Fat	115.84 g	14.48 g
Cholesterol	31.06 mg	3.883 mg
Dietary fibre	15.51 g	1.939 g
Sodium	1472.8 mg	184.1 mg
Iron	8.24 mg	1.03 mg

St Kitts and Nevis

Conch fritters

1 lb (454 g) conch meat
½ large onion, chopped
2 celery stalks
½ red pepper
½ green pepper
½ oz (14 g) seasoned salt
½ oz (14 g) garlic powder
1 egg
5 tbsp cornmeal
5 tbsp self-raising flour
1 tsp baking powder
4 tbsp buttermilk
a dash of hot pepper sauce
1 pint (560 ml) vegetable oil

1. Put the conch through a food grinder or food processor with the onion, celery and red and green peppers.
2. Add the salt, garlic powder and egg and mix well.
3. Mix the cornmeal, flour and baking powder and add to the conch mixture.
4. Add the buttermilk and hot sauce.
5. Heat the oil to 350°F.
6. Drop the mixture by heaped tablespoon into the oil and fry until light brown. Drain.

Serves: 15

Serve as a canapé with mayonnaise and lime juice or tartar sauce.

Nutrition information

	Per recipe	*Per serving*
Kilocalories	1957 kcal	130.5 kcal
Protein	190.3 g	12.7 g
Carbohydrate	171.9 g	11.46 g
Fat	48.86 g	3.26 g
Cholesterol	215.3 mg	14.35 mg
Dietary fibre	8.518 g	0.56 g
Sodium	3651 mg	243.4 mg
Iron	98.45 mg	6.56 mg

Lemons (see page 69)

Escoveitched fish

3 lb (1.36 kg) fish, sliced in ½-inch (1-cm) thick slices
2 or 3 limes or lemons
4 tsp black pepper and salt combined
¼ pint (140 ml) oil
1 pint (560 ml) cane or malt vinegar (white or brown)
2 large onions, sliced
½ scotch bonnet pepper, cut in strips, or ½ tsp dried tabasco pepper
1 tsp pimento seeds or whole allspice
½ tsp whole black peppercorns

1. Wash the fish in water to which the juice of the limes or lemons has been added. Dry thoroughly.
2. When absolutely dry, coat the fish on both sides with the combined salt and black pepper and set aside on paper towels.
3. Heat the oil in a frying pan to boiling point and fry the fish on both sides until crisp. Set the fish aside in a deep dish.
4. In a saucepan, combine the vinegar, sliced onions, pepper, pimento seeds and peppercorns, and bring to the boil. Simmer until the onions are tender.
5. Remove from the heat and cool.
6. Pour over the fish and leave steeping overnight.

Serves: 6

Recommended fish to use: snapper, jack, cutlass, sprats, goat fish. If using sprats or goat fish, leave the fish whole.

Nutrition information

	Per recipe	*Per serving*
Kilocalories	1972 kcal	328.7 kcal
Protein	285.8 g	47.63 g
Carbohydrate	67.99 g	11.33 g
Fat	61.05 g	10.18 g
Cholesterol	496.3 mg	82.71 mg
Dietary fibre	4.848 g	0.808 g
Sodium	9405 mg	1567.5 mg
Iron	7.925 mg	1.32 mg

Stuffed avocado salad

1 head of lettuce
2 cucumbers
2 avocados
2 tbsp lime juice
2 tbsp sweet pickle
4 oz (113 g) cooked peas or beans
¼ tsp black pepper
¼ tsp salt
2 oz (56 g) grated cheese
1 tomato
2 hard-boiled eggs, sliced
salad cream
2 tbsp chopped nuts

1. Wash the lettuce and put in a covered bowl in the refrigerator to chill.
2. Wash and slice the cucumbers and add salt to taste.
3. Cut the avocados in half lengthwise and peel off the skin.
4. Place the avocados in bowl, sprinkle with the lime juice and cover.
5. Mix together the pickle, peas and seasoning, and use to fill the hollows of the avocados.
6. Sprinkle with the cheese.
7. Cut the tomato into 8 wedges and place 2 on each avocado half.
8. Arrange the avocados on a bed of lettuce. Lay the sliced cucumber and slices of hard-boiled egg around the avocados.
9. Dot with salad cream and sprinkle with chopped nuts.

Serves: 4

Nutrition information

	Per recipe	*Per serving*
Kilocalories	1718 kcal	429.5 kcal
Protein	55.36 g	13.84 g
Carbohydrate	119.1 g	29.8 g
Fat	122.7 g	30.67 g
Cholesterol	485.9 mg	121.47 mg
Dietary fibre	47.26 g	11.81 g
Sodium	2555 mg	638.7 mg
Iron	11.44 mg	2.86 mg

Rikkita beef

8 oz (227 g) steak
2 garlic cloves
2 hot peppers, finely chopped
½ pint (280 ml) white wine or champagne
1 tsp curry powder
½ pint (280 ml) Italian dressing

1. Put the steak in a plastic bag with the garlic, half the chopped hot peppers and the wine and marinate for 1 hour. Remove from bag.
2. Put in a large pan with the curry powder and remaining hot pepper.
3. Simmer the meat for 45 minutes or until fully cooked.
4. Place the meat in a bowl, pour Italian dressing over, and serve.

Serves: 4

Nutrition information

	Per recipe	*Per serving*
Kilocalories	1872.4 kcal	468.1 kcal
Protein	42.48 g	10.62 g
Carbohydrate	31.16 g	7.792 g
Fat	159.6 g	39.92 g
Cholesterol	153.36 mg	38.34 mg
Dietary fibre	1.86 g	0.497 g
Sodium	1999.6 mg	499.9 mg
Iron	5.788 mg	1.447 mg

St Lucia

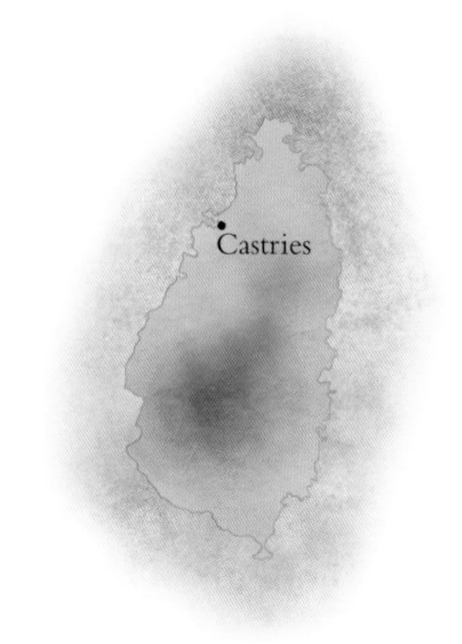

Labourer's lunch

(Jan coude mai marqe)

2 lb (908 g) each of salted beef and salted pork, cubed and soaked in water for 4 hours
2 lb (908 g) red kidney beans, soaked in water for 4 hours
2 lb (908 g) each of dasheen, yam, plantain, tannia, peeled and cubed
2 lb (908 g) flour
1 lb (454 g) butter or margarine
4 tbsp coconut oil
2 tsp black pepper
1 small sprig of thyme
1 lb (454 g) onions, sliced

1. Remove the meat and beans from the soaking water and wash several times. Place in a very deep saucepan. Add enough water to cover, and cook over a low heat for 3 hours, or until the beans are tender.
2. Meanwhile, cook together the dasheen, yams, plantain and tannia in salted water until tender (at least 30 minutes).
3. After the initial 3 hours of cooking put the flour in a wooden bowl, add enough salted water to make a workable dough, and roll the dough into thumb-sized pieces ½ inch (0.5 cm) thick. Add to the stewing meat one by one.
4. Check the dumplings to make sure that they are not sticking to the bottom of the pan. Then add the butter, oil, black pepper, thyme and onions. Cook slowly for 30 minutes, stirring occasionally.
5. When cooked, place the stew in a large bowl in the centre of the table, surrounded by the vegetables in separate dishes. Place a ladle in the stew for the labourers to serve themselves.

Serves: 12

This is a meal for hard-working labourers/farmers – hence the amount of vegetables.

Nutrition information

	Per recipe	*Per serving*
Kilocalories	19791 kcal	1649.25 kcal
Protein	577.7 g	48.14 g
Carbohydrate	1544 g	128.66 g
Fat	1265 g	105.41 g
Cholesterol	993.1 mg	82.75 mg
Dietary fibre	50.13 g	4.17 g
Sodium	3953 mg	329.41 mg
Iron	185.6 mg	15.46 mg

Dasheen

Stewed chicken dudon

2 tsp brown sugar
a whole chicken, cut into 8 pieces
½ tsp salt
1 sprig of thyme
1 tsp black pepper
4 tbsp coconut oil
8 oz (227 g) butter or margarine
2 lb (908 g) onions, sliced
4 garlic cloves, chopped
a 4-inch (10 cm) cinnamon stick
2 large tomatoes, cut into wedges
1 large sweet pepper, sliced
cornstarch or arrowroot (optional)

1. Melt the sugar in a very heavy pan. Stir constantly until it is black. Remove from the heat and cool.
2. Add, drop by drop, 2 tablespoons hot water. Stir over low heat until the burnt sugar becomes a thick, dark liquid.
3. Wash the chicken and season with the salt, thyme and pepper.
4. Put the oil and butter in a pan over high heat. Place the chicken in the pan and sprinkle with the onion, burnt sugar and garlic. Add the cinnamon stick, tomatoes and sweet pepper.
5. Reduce the heat to medium and add enough water to keep the chicken moist. Stir gently until well mixed.
6. If desired, thicken the gravy with a little cornstarch or arrowroot.
7. Cook for approximately 30 minutes, until the meat falls away from the leg bones.

Serves: 8

Serve with pigeon peas and rice.

Nutrition information

	Per recipe	***Per serving***
Kilocalories	5052.8 kcal	631.6 kcal
Protein	274.16 g	34.27 g
Carbohydrate	98.88 g	12.36 g
Fat	396.48 g	49.56 g
Cholesterol	912 mg	114 mg
Dietary fibre	17.48 g	2.186 g
Sodium	4420.8 mg	552.6 mg
Iron	17.2 mg	2.15 mg

Cassava pone

2 lb (908 g) cassava, grated
1 large dry coconut, grated
1 oz (28 g) butter
8 oz (227 g) sugar
1 tsp ground cloves
1 tsp mixed spice
1 tsp vanilla essence

1. Mix the cassava and coconut together.
2. Cut in the butter. Add the sugar and flavourings.
3. Add just enough water to bind.
4. Place in a greased pan and bake in a moderate oven, 350°F, for 40–45 minutes until crisp and brown.

Serves: 10

Nutrition information

	Per recipe	***Per serving***
Kilocalories	2967 kcal	296.7 kcal
Protein	14.64 g	1.46 g
Carbohydrate	597.2 g	59.72 g
Fat	66.55 g	6.65 g
Cholesterol	62.13 mg	6.21 mg
Dietary fibre	5.473 g	0.54 g
Sodium	627.2 mg	62.72 mg
Iron	13.2 mg	1.32 mg

St Vincent and the Grenadines

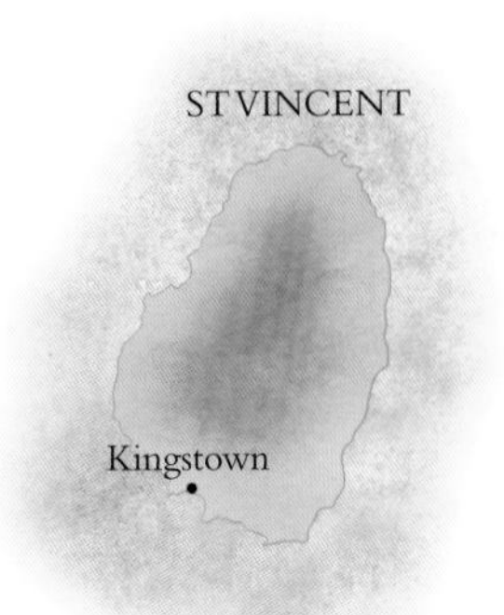

Stuffed jacks

1½ lb (681 g) jacks (6)
1 tbsp lime juice
½ tsp salt
2 tbsp local seasoning
2 oz (56 g) flour
oil for frying
lime to garnish

For the farine stuffing:
4 oz (113 g) farine
1 tbsp margarine
4 tbsp chopped seasoning (onion, chive, sweet pepper, parsley, thyme, garlic)
½ tsp salt
½ tsp white pepper
1 tbsp tomato ketchup

1. Clean the fish and marinate in the lime juice and salt. Rub with seasoning.
2. Make the stuffing. Soak the farine in ½ pint (280 ml) water for about 5 minutes. Melt the margarine, add the soaked farine and the other stuffing ingredients and cook for about 3 minutes.
3. Stuff the fish with the farine stuffing.
4. Dredge the fish in flour.
5. Fry in hot oil until brown.
6. Serve garnished with lime.

Serves: 6

The farine stuffing can also be used for stuffing meats.

Nutrition information

	Per recipe	***Per serving***
Kilocalories	1997 kcal	332.83 kcal
Protein	149.6 g	24.93 g
Carbohydrate	90.51 g	15.08 g
Fat	111.4 g	18.56 g
Cholesterol	320.2 mg	53.36 mg
Dietary fibre	4.048 g	0.67 g
Sodium	3182 mg	530.33 mg
Iron	15.76 mg	2.62 mg

Green banana mince pie

3 lb (1.4 kg) green bananas
2 tsp salt
2 tsp lime juice
1 onion
2 celery stalks
1 lb (454 g) minced meat
2 oz (56 g) margarine
2 oz (56 g) breadcrumbs
1 egg
6 fl oz (210 ml) milk

1. Peel the bananas and cook in boiling water, adding 1 teaspoon salt and the lime juice.
2. Mince the onion and celery.
3. Sauté the meat with the onion, celery and the rest of the salt in half the margarine. Cook for 8–10 minutes. Stir in the breadcrumbs.
4. Cut the cooked bananas into ¼-inch (0.5-cm) slices.
5. Divide the bananas into four portions and the meat into three portions.
6. Arrange a portion of bananas in the bottom of a greased ovenproof dish, then a portion of meat. Repeat the arrangement, ending with a layer of bananas on top.
7. Beat the egg and milk together, pour over the mixture and dot with the remaining margarine.
8. Bake at 350°F for 30 minutes until brown.
9. If desired, garnish with slices of hard-boiled egg or tomato.

Serves: 6

Nutrition information

	Per recipe	***Per serving***
Kilocalories	3728 kcal	621.33 kcal
Protein	114.8 g	19.13 g
Carbohydrate	445.2 g	74.2 g
Fat	182.4 g	30.4 g
Cholesterol	623.6 mg	103.93 mg
Dietary fibre	11.35 g	1.89 g
Sodium	5771 mg	961.8 mg
Iron	23.38 mg	3.896 mg

Madungo dumplings

1 lb (454 g) madungo
6 oz (168 g) grated coconut
2 oz (56 g) sugar
½ tsp cinnamon
a pinch of salt
1 oz (28 g) lard
1 oz (28 g) margarine
1 tsp baking soda
2–4 oz (56–113 g) flour
oil for frying

1. Dampen the madungo with cold water and put into about 1 pint (560 ml) boiling water. Scald for 10 minutes.
2. Remove the madungo from the water and reserve the water. Take off the jelly-like covering and crush both with a wooden spoon while still warm.
3. Add the coconut, sugar, cinnamon, salt, lard and margarine.
4. Dissolve the baking soda in about 4 tablespoons of the reserved water, and add to the mixture.
5. Add enough flour to make a soft dough and knead well. Divide into 10–12 small pieces and shape into round dumplings.
6. Fry in hot oil or wrap in pieces of banana leaves and bake on a hot copper.

Makes: about 12

Nutrition information

	Per recipe	*Per serving*
Kilocalories	2018 kcal	168.16 kcal
Protein	23.97 g	1.99 g
Carbohydrate	284.7 g	23.72 g
Fat	93.51 g	7.79 g
Cholesterol	15.9 mg	1.32 mg
Dietary fibre	33 g	2.75 g
Sodium	1908 mg	159 mg
Iron	10.83 mg	0.90 mg

Suriname

Nasi goreng

1 lb 5 oz (600 g) rice
2 tbsp margarine or oil
8 blades of eschallot, chopped
2 garlic cloves, chopped
1 piece trassi, chopped
3½ oz (100 g) shrimps
10½ oz (300 g) ham or pieces of meat
1 tbsp tomato ketchup
1 tbsp ketoember
djintan
2 eggs

1. Boil the rice.
2. Heat 1 tablespoon of margarine or oil in a heavy pot and fry together the eschallot, garlic and trassi.
3. Add the shrimps, meat, ketchup, ketoember, djintan and pepper to taste and continue to fry.
4. Add the rice and cook until the mixture becomes golden brown.
5. Make an omelette with the eggs and remaining margarine or oil.
6. Cut the omelette into strips and garnish the dish.

Serves: 8

Nutrition information

	Per recipe	*Per serving*
Kilocalories	4759.57 kcal	594.94 kcal
Protein	88.6 g	11.07 g
Carbohydrate	499.92 g	62.49 g
Fat	70.26 g	8.78 g
Cholesterol	673.5 mg	84.18 mg
Dietary fibre	1.14 g	0.14 g
Sodium	4458.7 mg	557.3 mg
Iron	9.87 mg	1.23 mg

Peanut soup

2 lb 3 oz (1 kg) chicken, cut into pieces
3 celery stalks
1 onion
1 green plantain, cooked (see method)
2 oz (56 g) peanut butter
3 tomatoes
3 bouillon cubes

1. Bring 2½ pints (1.5 litres) water to the boil.
2. Add the chicken, 1 celery stalk and ½ onion and cook slowly.
3. Mash the cooked plantain while hot and mix with the peanut butter and some warm water.
4. Add the plantain mixture to the cooking broth and stir. Cook slowly.
5. Chop the tomatoes and the remaining celery and onion and add to the soup.
6. Taste the soup and add bouillon cubes to flavour, together with pepper, if desired.

Serves: 6

This soup is usually served with foo foo, made from plantains.

Nutrition information

	Per recipe	*Per serving*
Kilocalories	3887 kcal	647.84 kcal
Protein	214.04 g	35.67 g
Carbohydrate	390.81 g	65.14 g
Fat	178.19 g	29.59 g
Cholesterol	900 mg	150 mg
Dietary fibre	20.58 g	3.43 g
Sodium	6876.2 mg	1146.5 mg
Iron	21.77 mg	3.63 mg

Trinidad and Tobago

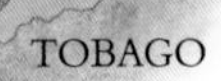

Bul jol

8 oz (227 g) salted cod fish
2 tomatoes, sliced
1 small onion, chopped
½ red pepper
1 tbsp salad oil
juice of 1 lime
lettuce leaves
4 avocado slices
a few blades of chive, chopped

1. Soak the fish in cold water to remove some salt.
2. Clean and shred it.
3. Mix the tomatoes, onion and pepper in a bowl with the fish.
4. Sprinkle with the oil and lime juice to marinate.
5. Serve in small plates on lettuce leaves, garnished with an avocado slice and a few pieces of chive.

Serves: 4

Nutrition information

	Per recipe	***Per serving***
Kilocalories	2241 kcal	560.2 kcal
Protein	413.2 g	103.3 g
Carbohydrate	30.79 g	7.69 g
Fat	43.37 g	10.83 g
Cholesterol	985.8 mg	246.45 mg
Dietary fibre	8.294 g	2.073 g
Sodium	45619 mg	11404.75 mg
Iron	18.26 mg	4.565 mg

Sancoche

4 oz (113 g) salted meat or a ham bone ('salt kine')
2–3 crabs
12 young eddo, dasheen or callaloo leaves
8–10 young ochroes
2 garlic cloves
1 onion
1 blade of chive ('sive')
1 sprig of thyme
1 celery stalk (optional)
salt and black pepper to taste
1 tbsp butter
1 pint (560 ml) thick coconut milk
1 lb (454 g) pumpkin
1 whole red hot pepper (not bruised, stem intact)

1. Soak the salted meat and cut into small pieces.
2. Scrub and scald the crabs.
3. Strip the stalks and mid-ribs from the leaves. Wash, roll and shred finely.
4. Wash and cut up the ochroes and seasonings.
5. Put all the ingredients into a saucepan with the whole pepper on top, and simmer until everything is tender.
6. Remove the pepper, meat and crabs.
7. Purée the remaining mixture using a swizzle or a blender.
8. Replace the meat.
9. Pour into a serving dish, place the crabs on top and garnish with the whole pepper.

Serves: 4

Nutrition information

	Per recipe	*Per serving*
Kilocalories	2533 kcal	633.25 kcal
Protein	142.5 g	35.62 g
Carbohydrate	94.33 g	23.58 g
Fat	190.4 g	47.6 g
Cholesterol	603.3 mg	150.82 mg
Dietary fibre	19.46 g	4.86 g
Sodium	4240 mg	1060 mg
Iron	24.86 mg	6.21 mg

Blue crabs

Trinidad peas and rice

8 oz (227 g) salted or fresh pork
1 lb (454 g) pigeon peas or any other peas
1 tsp salt
2 pints (1.1 litres) water, stock or coconut milk
1 tbsp cooking oil
1 small onion, chopped
½ sweet pepper, chopped
2 tomatoes, chopped
1 sprig of parsley
1 sprig of thyme
1 blade of chive
8 oz (227 g) rice

1. If using salted pork, soak overnight.
2. Cut up the meat and cook with the peas and salt in half the water, stock or coconut milk.
3. Heat the oil and brown the onion, pepper, tomatoes, parsley, thyme and chive.
4. When the peas are almost cooked, add the remaining liquid, the rice and browned seasoning. Simmer until tender.

Serves: 6

Nutrition information

	Per recipe	*Per serving*
Kilocalories	3460 kcal	576.66 kcal
Protein	140.4 g	23.4 g
Carbohydrate	373.6 g	62.26 g
Fat	163.7 g	27.28 g
Cholesterol	146.1 mg	24.35 mg
Dietary fibre	3.966 g	0.66 g
Sodium	2428 mg	404.6 mg
Iron	27.23 mg	4.53 mg

Sweet peppers

Pastelles

2 oz (56 g) shortening
1½ lb (681 g) grated corn
1½ lb (681 g) minced beefsteak
2 large onions, chopped
3 tbsp dripping
4 oz (113 g) olives, chopped
2 oz (56 g) capers, chopped
1 green pepper, chopped
8 oz (227 g) raisins
2 large fig leaves

1. Stir the shortening into the corn. Place in a large bowl and add enough boiling water to mix to a smooth paste. Set aside until cool enough to handle.
2. Shape heaped tablespoons of the mixture into 24 balls.
3. Sauté the meat and onion in the dripping.
4. When almost done, add the olives, capers and green pepper and remove from the heat.
5. Stir in the raisins.
6. Wipe the fig leaves and heat them over a flame to make them pliable.
7. Cut each leaf into 12 squares. Grease the centre of each square with shortening.
8. Place a corn ball in the centre and flatten to ⅛ inch (0.3 cm).
9. Place a portion of the meat mixture in the centre of each corn ball.
10. Roll and fold over the ends of the leaves to form an envelope.
11. Tie into a parcel with cotton string and steam over boiling water for 30–60 minutes.
12. Either serve the pastelles in the fig leaves or remove the leaves before serving.

Makes: 24

Nutrition information

	Per recipe	*Per serving*
Kilocalories	6839 kcal	284.9 kcal
Protein	296.9 g	12.37 g
Carbohydrate	883.7 g	36.82 g
Fat	248.5 g	11.85 g
Cholesterol	737.7 mg	30.73 mg
Dietary fibre	123.5 g	5.14 g
Sodium	2201 mg	91.70 mg
Iron	50.27 mg	2.09 mg

Part 2

An Invitation to Adventure

Flavour aids

Herbs

The fragrant leaves of any of various annual or perennial plants that grow in temperate zones and do not have woody stems. Herbs can be purchased in dried or fresh forms and can be found at various times of the year, depending on the herb. Choose herbs that have a clean fresh fragrance and a bright colour, without any sign of wilting or browning. They can be stored in the refrigerator, wrapped in a barely damp paper towel and sealed airtight in a plastic bag, for up to 5 days.

Dried herbs are available year-round in metal or cardboard boxes, bottles, cellophane packages and unglazed ceramic pots. They have a stronger, more concentrated flavour than fresh herbs, but quickly lose their pungency. Crushed or ground herbs become lacklustre more quickly than whole herbs. The more airtight the storage container, the longer the herbs will last.

Spices

Pungent or aromatic seasonings that are obtained from the bark, buds, fruit, roots, seeds or stems of various plants and trees, whereas herbs usually come from the leafy part of a plant. Many spices are available in both whole and ground forms. Ground spices quickly lose their aroma and flavour, so it is wise to buy them in small quantities. Whole spices can be ground as needed. Store spices in airtight containers in a cool, dark place for no more than 6 months. Spices are used to enhance a wide variety of food, both sweet and savoury. They should be used sparingly so they do not overpower the foods being seasoned.

Allspice (*Pimenta dioica*) [pimento]
Allspice is from berries which have a taste of cinnamon, cloves and nutmeg combined. The small aromatic seeds can be used whole or ground, but are best used freshly ground. It is used for flavouring marinades, sauces, pickles, stews, soups, chocolate, fruit salads and spicy hot tea. In Caribbean cuisine, allspice, with its pleasing clove-like aroma, is the most important and extensively used spice. Meat is often stuffed with allspice leaves and barbecued over a fire of allspice wood.

Almond (*Prunus amygdalus*)
There are two main types of almond – sweet and bitter. The flavour of **sweet**

almonds is delicate and slightly sweet. They are readily available in markets and are used in cooking. The more strongly flavoured **bitter almonds** contain traces of lethal prussic acid when raw. Processed bitter almonds are used to flavour **almond extract**, which is produced by combining bitter-almond oil with ethyl alcohol. The flavour is very intense, so the extract should be used with care.

Basil (*Ocimum basilicum*)
The leaves and, frequently, the entire herb are harvested. The best harvesting season is before flowering. Basil leaves should always be used fresh, as they lose most of their flavour within a few weeks after drying. Mediterranean basil is one of the most pleasant herbs, and indispensable for several Mediterranean cuisines. The sweet and aromatic fragrance is especially popular in Italy. Since the delicate aroma of basil is quickly destroyed by cooking, chopped basil leaves are frequently sprinkled over cold or warm dishes just before serving.

Bay leaf (*Laurus nobilis*) [bay laurel, laurel leaf]
This herb comes from the evergreen bay laurel tree, native to the Mediterranean. The aromatic leaves are used in stews, spiced vinegars, soups, gravies, savoury rice, salad dressing, marinades, pastas, condiments and porridges, and with poultry, pork and fish. They are generally removed before serving. Overuse of this herb can make a dish bitter. Fresh bay leaves are seldom available in markets. Dried bay leaves, which have a fraction of the flavour of the fresh leaves, can be found in supermarkets. Store dried bay leaves airtight in a cool, dark place for up to 6 months.

Bouquet garni
A bunch of herbs (the classic trio being parsley, thyme and bay leaf) that are either tied together or placed in a cheesecloth bag and used to flavour soups, stews and broths. Tying or bagging the herbs allows for their easy removal before the dish is served.

Chive [*Allium schoenoprasum*]
Related to the onion and leek, chive has slender, vivid green, hollow stems. Chives have a mild onion flavour and are available fresh year-round. Look for those with a uniform green colour and no signs of wilting or browning. Store in a plastic bag in the refrigerator for up to a week. Fresh chives can be snipped with scissors to the desired length. They should

be added towards the end of the cooking time to retain their flavour. Both chives and their edible lavender flowers are a tasty and colourful addition to salads. Frozen and freeze-dried chives are also available in most supermarkets. Chives are a good source of Vitamin A and also contain a fair amount of potassium and calcium.

Cinnamon (*Cinnamomum verum*)
Cinnamon bark, whole or ground, is a popular household spice used internationally. It is used to flavour beverages like hot chocolate, cocoa and juices. It is used in baked goods, cakes, biscuits, puddings, cereals, sweet sauces, jams and jellies, pickles, relishes, vinegars, soups and gravies, and can be either mixed with tea or used alone as a spicy tea.

Citron (*Citrus aurantium*) [candied peel]
The citron looks like a large, yellow-green, lumpy lemon. This fruit is grown for its extremely thick peel, which is candied and used in baking. Candied citron can be purchased fresh in specialist foodstores, or with preservatives in supermarkets. Either should be stored in the freezer for maximum freshness. Candied citron halves are sometimes available, but it is more likely to be found chopped or in strips.

Clove (*Syzygium aromaticum*)
Clove is the common name for a tropical small to medium-sized evergreen tree of the myrtle family, and for its dried flower buds. The clove tree is a native to the Moluccas in eastern Indonesia, and is now cultivated elsewhere in the tropics. In Grenada, great amounts of cloves are grown and exported throughout the world. Cloves are also used for cooking in every household. This dried flavoured flower bud is used at home, whole or ground, to season hams, sausages, meats, mincemeat pies, fish, preserves and pickles, and in condiments, relishes, gravies, soups, sauces and desserts. It adds a subtle flavour to sorrel drink and alcoholic drinks.

Coriander (*Coriandrum sativum*)
The fruits and leaves possess totally different flavours and can therefore not be substituted for one another. Drying destroys most of the leaves' fragrance, yet dried coriander leaves are mentioned in some recipes. The plants grow leaves of two different shapes: the base leaves are broad, similar to Italian (flat-leaved) parsley and are reputed to have the better flavour. Leaves attached to the stems are pinnate and their flavour is said to be less fresh.

Coriander seeds are an essential part of curry powder and Indian masalas, especially in the garam masala of northern India.

Cumin (*Cuminum cyminum*) [gheera]
Cumin is a popular spice all over the world, especially in Latin America,

North Africa and all over Asia, but less so in Europe, where its use is restricted to flavouring cheese in the Netherlands and in France. Cumin is one of the most typical spices of India, especially the southern part. The fruits are used whole, and are fried or dry-roasted before use. The seeds form an important part of curry powder and of another important Indian spice mixture, garam masala. Cumin is also essential in the preparation of northern Indian tandoori dishes. The fragrance of roasted cumin, typically in combination with coriander, is the most characteristic impression from south Indian or Sri Lankan cuisine.

Djintan

Djintan is made of the seeds of the tropical cumin. It smells fresh and does not have a savoury flavour. It is used in both rice dishes and sauces. It is usually used together with ketoembar. Use 1 teaspoon of djintan with 2 teaspoons of ketoembar. If a recipe mentions fresh djintan, the same amount of dried product can be used. The five basic herbs of the Indonesian kitchen are: ketoembar, djintan, djahe, koenjit and laos.

Garlic (*Allium sativum*)

The bulb is the part of the plant that is used; there is minimum use for fresh garlic leaves. It has a strong and characteristic odour which is markedly different in the fresh and dried states. The use of fried or cooked garlic is common. On heating, the pungency and strong odour get lost and the aroma becomes more subtle and less dominant, harmonizing perfectly with ginger, pepper, chillies and many other spices. It is, therefore, an essential ingredient for nearly every cuisine of the world. Raw garlic may also be pickled in vinegar or olive oil. Since some of its aroma is extracted by the liquid, pickled garlic is usually very mild. Herbal vinegar is commonly made with 1 or 2 garlic cloves per 1¾ pints (1 litre) vinegar.

Ginger (*Zingiber officinale*)

The name ginger comes from the Sanskrit word for 'horn root', undoubtedly referring to its knobbly appearance. It has a tan skin and a flesh that ranges in colour from pale greenish yellow to ivory. The flavour is peppery and slightly sweet, while the aroma is pungent and spicy. Many people like raw ginger, and this is the form most popular in South East

Asia: fresh ginger is grated or finely chopped, may be soaked in water for several hours, and is then added to the dish not long before serving. This kind of use results in a fresh, spicy and pungent taste. If fresh ginger is cooked, the flavour increases in pungency but decreases in freshness.

The flavour of **dried ground ginger** is very different from that of its fresh form and it is not an appropriate substitute in dishes that specify fresh ginger. It is, however, delicious in many savoury dishes and indispensable in sweets like gingerbread and gingersnaps and in many spice cookies.

Ketoembar

Ketoembar is made of the seeds of the coriander. It has a pleasant, mild flavour and smells sweet. It is used in every Asian country, usually together with djintan (cumin), in the proportion one-third djintan to two-thirds ketoembar. Fresh ketoembar can be replaced by the same amount of dried ketoembar.

Mace (*Myristica fragrans*)

Fresh mace is a bright red net-like membrane (arils) wrapped around a dark brown and brittle shell, within which is a single aromatic seed (nutmeg). On drying, mace changes from red to yellowish orange. Mace whole or ground is used for seasoning soups, sauces (wine and fruit sauces), stews, pickles and for seafoods. It has a mild nutmeg-like flavour and is used for baked goods, cakes, doughnuts and cookies. Powdered mace sprinkled on cooked cabbage masks the sulphide odours.

Mangrile [black onion seeds, kala jeera, kalunji, nigella]

This Indian spice looks like small roundish dark brown/black seeds, like black sesame seeds. It is used in making achar and stuffed fried carila (carailli). Also used to make garam masala.

Mustard (*Brassica alba*)

Mustard seeds are sold whole, ground into powder or processed further into prepared mustard. **Powdered mustard** is simply finely ground mustard seed. Mustard seeds can be stored for up to a year in a dry, dark place, and powdered mustard for about 6 months. Whole seeds are used for pickling, flavouring cooked meats and vegetables, and as a source for freshly ground mustard. Powdered mustards and freshly ground seeds are used in sauces, as a seasoning in main dishes and as an ingredient in salad dressings.

Prepared mustard is generally made from powdered mustard combined with seasonings and a liquid such as water, vinegar, wine or beer. American-style prepared mustard is a mild mixture made from the less pungent white seed flavoured with sugar, vinegar and turmeric to make it yellow. It adds flavour to mild cheeses. European and Chinese prepared mustards are made from brown seeds and are much zestier and more flavourful. The German prepared mustards can range from very hot to sweet and mild. Chinese mustards are usually the hottest and most pungent of the prepared mustards. Unopened, prepared mustard can be stored in a cool, dark place for about 2 years; once opened, it should be refrigerated.

Nutmeg (*Myristica fragrans*)
Nutmeg is one of the old, great spices. Both nutmeg and mace are the products of one fruit from the nutmeg tree. The fruit resembles a small peach or apricot, but in place of soft juicy flesh there is a thick fibrous husk underneath the skin of the nutmeg fruit. Inside this husk is a thin layer of lacy material (arils) that is the spice called mace. The mace surrounds the seed shell which contains the nutmeg seed. A pinch of grated nutmeg gives a delicious spicy flavour to egg nogs, milk drinks, rum punches, spiced hot wines, puddings and custards, salads, roasted lamb and sweet sauces.

Onion (*Allium sepa*)
Related to the lily, this underground bulb is prized around the world for its pungent flavour and odour. There are two main classifications of onion: **green onions**, also called eschallots or scallions, and **dry onions**, which are simply mature onions with a juicy flesh covered with dry, papery skin. Dry onions come in a wide range of sizes, shapes and flavours. Tiny pearl onions are mild-flavoured and about the size of a small marble. They can be cooked and served as a side dish or pickled and used as a condiment or garnish. Boiling onions are about 1 inch (2.5 cm) in diameter and mildly flavoured.

Choose onions that are heavy for their size with dry, papery skins with no signs of spotting or moistness. Avoid onions with soft spots. Store in a cool, dry place with good air circulation for up to 2 months. Onions contain a fair amount of Vitamin C with traces of other vitamins and minerals.

Parsley (*Petroselium sativum*)
This slightly peppery, fresh-flavoured herb is commonly used as a flavouring and garnish. Though there are more than 30 varieties of this herb, the most popular are curly-leaf parsley and the more strongly flavoured Italian or flat-leaf parsley. Fresh curly-leaf parsley is widely available year-round, while Italian parsley must sometimes be searched out in gourmet produce markets.

Parsley is sold in bunches and should be chosen with bright green leaves that show no sign of wilting. Wash fresh parsley, shaking off excess moisture, and wrap first in paper towels, then in a plastic bag. Refrigerate for up to a week. Dried parsley is available in the spice section of most supermarkets but its flavour bears little resemblance to that of fresh. Parsley is an excellent source of Vitamins A and C.

Parsley

Pepper (*Piper nigrum*)
The world's most popular spice is a berry that grows in grapelike clusters on the pepper plant, a climbing vine native to India and Indonesia. The berry is processed to produce three basic types of peppercorn – black, white and green. The most common is the **black peppercorn**, which is picked when the berry is not quite ripe, then dried until it shrivels and the skin turns from dark brown to black. It's the strongest flavoured of the three – slightly hot with a hint of sweetness. The less pungent **white peppercorn** has been allowed to ripen, after which the skin is removed and the berry is dried. The result is a smaller, smoother skinned, light-tan berry with a milder flavour. White pepper is used to a great extent for appearance, usually in light-coloured sauces or foods where dark specks of black pepper would stand out. The **green peppercorn** is the soft, under-ripe berry that's usually preserved in brine. It has a fresh flavour that's less pungent than the berry in its other forms. Black and white peppercorns are available whole, cracked, and coarsely or finely ground. Whole peppercorns freshly ground with a pepper mill deliver more flavour than pre-ground pepper, which loses its flavour comparatively quickly. Whole dried peppercorns can be stored in a cool, dark place for about a year; ground pepper will keep its flavour for about 4 months.

Peppermint (*Mentha piperita*)
There are over 30 species of mint, the two most popular and widely available being peppermint and spearmint. **Peppermint** is the more pungent of the two. It has bright green leaves, purple-tinged stems and a peppery flavour. Mint is used in both sweet and savoury dishes and in drinks. Mint is available fresh, dried, as an extract, and in the form of **oil of spearmint** or **oil of peppermint**, both highly concentrated flavourings. Most forms can usually be found in supermarkets.

Saffron (*Crocus sativus Linneaus*)
The saffron filaments are actually the dried stigmas of the saffron crocus flower. Each flower contains only three stigmas. These filaments must be picked from each flower by hand, and more than 75,000 of the flowers are needed to produce just one pound of saffron filaments, making saffron the world's most precious and expensive spice. However, because of the strong colouring power and intense flavour of saffron, this spice must be used sparingly. As a spice it is used for its bright orange-yellow colouring and flavour-improving intense aroma. Saffron is added to cheese products, such as cottage cheese and Parmesan, to soups, chicken and meat, various spirits, pasta and rice. To use saffron, either infuse a few threads in a cup of hot water and add the coloured liquid towards the end of cooking, or crumble the threads and add directly to the pot.

Sage (*Salvia officinalis*)
Sage is a perennial that grows to about 2–3 feet (60–90 cm). It flourishes best in a sunny area and loose soil. It is another herb from the Mediterranean. Sage is part of the mint family, Lamiaceae, and has the typical square stems of that family. It has a strong flavour when used in cooking, so should be added sparingly. Sage has been used in dressings by many people but it has a lot of other uses. It helps to preserve cheese and meats, so has been used in sausage and other meat preparations over the years.

Shallot (*Allium ascalonicum*)
Shallots are formed more like garlic than onions, with a head composed of multiple cloves, each covered with a thin, papery skin. The skin colour can vary from pale brown to pale grey to rose, and the off-white flesh is usually faintly tinged with green or purple. The two main types of shallots are the Jersey or 'false' shallot (the larger of the two) and the more subtly flavoured 'true' shallot. Fresh **green shallots** are available in the spring but, as with garlic and onions, **dry shallots** (i.e. with dry skins and moist flesh) are available year-round. Choose dry-skinned shallots that are plump and firm; there should be no sign of wrinkling or sprouting. Refrigerate fresh shallots for up to a week. Store dry shallots in a cool, dry, well-ventilated place for up to a month. Freeze-dried and dehydrated forms are also available. Shallots are favoured for their mild onion flavour and can be used in the same manner as onions.

Thyme (*Thymus vulgaris*)
There are several varieties of this member of the mint family, Lamiaceae, a perennial herb native to southern Europe and the Mediterranean. Both leaves and, frequently, the whole herb (leaves plus stem) are sold. Whatever the variety, thyme is widely used in cooking to add flavour to vegetables, meat, poultry and fish dishes, soups and cream sauces. It's a basic herb of French cuisine and integral to **bouquet garni**.

Trassi [balachan, blachan]
A popular flavouring in the cuisines of Southeast Asian countries such as Malaysia, Burma and Indonesia, trassi is made from shrimp, sardines and other small salted fish that have been allowed to ferment in the sun until very pungent and odorous. It's then mashed and in some cases dried. Balachan is available in paste, powder or cake form in Asian markets.

Vanilla (*Vanilla planifolia*)
This long thin pod is the fruit of a luminous celadon-coloured orchid, which of over 20,000 orchid varieties is the only one that bears anything edible. The vanilla bean was once considered an aphrodisiac, and was so rare that it was reserved for royalty. **Vanilla extract** is the most common form of vanilla used today. It's made by macerating chopped beans in an alcohol–water solution in order to extract the flavour. The mixture is then aged for several months. The resulting brown liquid is clear and richly fragrant. There are double- and triple-strength vanilla extracts, as well as a **vanilla essence** – so strong that only a drop or two is needed.

Unique tastes

Casareep
Casareep is the juice of the cassava boiled until it reduces and caramelizes. It is of Amerindian origin and is made from the poisonous juice of the grated bitter cassava. The juice is boiled long and slowly, which removes the poison. The resulting thick brown liquid, casareep, is used to make pepperpot. The casareep not only gives the dish its distinctive flavour but also acts as a preservative. Thus the pepperpot can be kept for quite some time without spoiling. In Guyana, this is eaten with cassava bread, yeast bread, rice or foo foo (pounded green plantain balls).

Farine
This is made from the substance that remains after the cassava juice has been removed. This substance is sifted and is then parched in a heated flat pan until a light brown in colour. The finished product resembles coarse grains. It is another form in which cassava is used by the Amerindians as a staple.

Jerk
The ingredients of a good jerk paste are usually eschallots, ginger, thyme, garlic, cinnamon, peppercorns, nutmeg, pimento and, of course, scotch bonnet peppers.

OPPOSITE: *Pimentos*

Versatile vegetables

Although one of the most nutritious food items, vegetables are not always popular with young children and adults. Also, often when vegetables are used the method of preparation wastes the nutrients: the vegetables are cooked for long periods in large amounts of water, resulting in leaching out of the water-soluble nutrients. Some vegetables have less nutrients than others, e.g. cucumber and christophene. While vegetables can be low in energy, minerals and vitamins they do add fibre to the diet.

Coloured vegetables

In the Caribbean the vegetable foods are classified as a separate group called the coloured vegetables. The more popular foods within this group are spinach, callaloo, dasheen leaves, carrots and pumpkin. The major nutrients found in this group are:

Vitamin C
Vitamin A
Vitamin B group
Iron

ABOVE: *Cabbages* BELOW: *Cauliflowers*

Cabbage (*Brassica oleracea var. capitata*)
Cabbage is a thick-leaf green vegetable which grows with its pale green leaves folded in to form a 'head'. The leaves of some varieties are loose but others are compact and form various-shaped heads. The varieties range in colour from pale green through other darker shades of green, through to magenta red and purple. Most varieties have smooth leaves, but the Savoy types have crinkly textured leaves. Cabbage is praised for its ability to protect against certain types of cancer. Cabbage, Brussels sprouts and cauliflower are members of the cruciferous family – they fight against cancer by trapping certain carcinogens before they can do damage to the body. Cabbage is also a rich source of

Vitamin C, which plays a role against cancer as well as boosting the immune system.

Carrot (*Daucus carota*)
Carrots help to protect against cancer, boost the immune system and improve night vision. The fibre can reduce the risk of haemorrhoids, and few nutrients are lost during cooking. Crunching on raw carrots can tone and strengthen the gums. Serve carrots with raisins, in salads, stews or carrot pudding. Carrots were originally purple, but in the early 17th century orange varieties were developed.

They are a root vegetable but do not provide much starch and are best known for their Vitamin A and sugar content.

Cucumber (*Cucumis sativus*)
This is a member of the gourd family and there are several varieties which grow under tropical conditions. The fruit is dark green and cylindrical with tapering ends. It is usually between 6 and 12 inches (15 and 30 cm) in length. Cucumbers are generally eaten raw in salads but the more mature ones may be cooked in the same manner as squash. Unpeeled cucumbers are higher in nutritional value, as fibre and Vitamin A are lost by peeling.

Eggplant (*Solanum melongena*) [antrober, aubergine, boulanger, garden egg, melongene]
The eggplant is a member of the nightshade family, and is related to the potato and tomato. Though commonly thought of as a vegetable, eggplant is actually a fruit – specifically a berry. There are many varieties of this delicious food, ranging in colour from rich purple to white, in length from 2 to 12 inches (5 to 30 cm) and in shape from oblong to round.

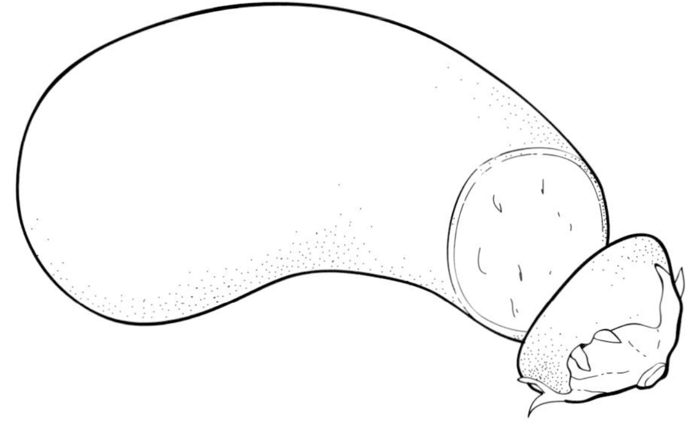

Eggplants become bitter with age and are very perishable. When young, the skin of most eggplants is deliciously edible; older eggplants should be peeled. Since the flesh discolours rapidly, an eggplant should be cut just before using. In general, eggplants have very little nutritive value on their own as they contain approximately 91% water.

This food can be prepared in a variety of ways, including baking, broiling and frying. It does, however, have a sponge-like capacity to soak up oil so it should be well coated with a batter or crumb mixture to inhibit fat absorption. Coated with a peas batter it makes a delicious Indian fritter called 'baigani'.

Green leafy vegetables

Callaloo (*Amaranthus*) [dasheen leaves, poi]

Cassava and sweet potato leaves

Mustard greens (*Brassica juncea*)

A member of the cruciferous vegetable family, mustard contains large amounts of beta carotene and Vitamin C that are important antioxidants. Mustard greens also contain a significant amount of iron and are a source of calcium that can be important to lactose-intolerant individuals.

Pakchoy (*Brassica pekinensis*) [bok choy]

Pumpkin leaves

Spinach (*Spinicia oleracea*) [bhaji, chaya]

Callaloo, pakchoy, spinach and dasheen leaves are excellent sources of carotenoids – the anti-cancer dietary factors. These green leafy vegetables also

Callaloo/dasheen leaves

Pakchoy

contain Vitamin C and B vitamins that help boost immunity. There is a good amount of blood pressure-lowering, bone-strengthening calcium and potassium, and ample fibre present in the leaves.

Lettuce

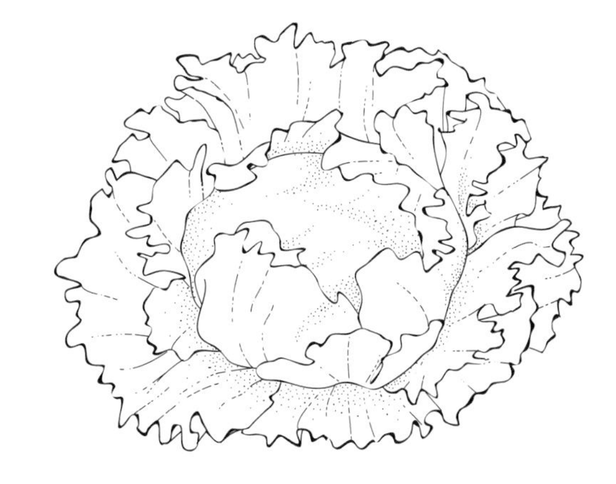

Lettuce is a fairly hardy, cool-weather vegetable that thrives when the average daily temperature is between 60 and 70°F (15 and 20°C). Primarily it is served raw in salads. Nutritionally it consists of approximately 94% water but it provides some calcium and potassium.

Ochro (*Abelmoschus esculentus*)

[lady's fingers, okra]

It is believed that this vegetable was introduced from Africa. It is a finger-shaped pod with a bright green colour and small light pink seeds. In cooking, it is very mucilaginous so it is recommended that a few drops of vinegar be added to the cooking water to reduce this and that salt should be added at the end of cooking. Young ochroes are best as they become fibrous when they mature. Ochroes are a fair source of calcium and potassium.

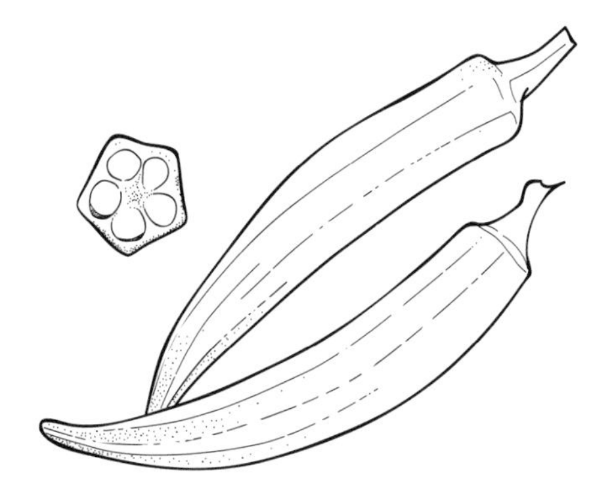

Pumpkin (*Cucurbita maxima*)

Large, round and orange, the pumpkin is a member of the gourd family, which also includes melon and squash. The flesh is orange and has a mild, sweet flavour. The seeds are delicately nutty when roasted. Whole pumpkins can be stored at room temperature for up to a month or in the refrigerator for up to 3 months. Pumpkin may be prepared in a variety of ways. It's a good source of Vitamin A and is one of the most abundant sources of cancer-fighting carotenoids. It also contains fibre, potassium and Vitamin C.

Christophenes

Squash (*Cucurbita pepo*)
Squashes are members of the gourd family. They are of varying colours, shapes and sizes. Some which are popular in the Caribbean include: yellow squash, zucchini, butternut squash and christophene. Squash is pleasantly mild and does not require prolonged cooking or it is reduced to mush. On its own, squash does not have any significant nutritive value as it is over 90% water. However, the butternut squash, which is pear-shaped and a deep orange in colour, is rich in beta carotene and provides a significant amount of fibre.

String bean (*Phaseolus vulgaris*)
[bodi, bora, cowpea, snap bean, yardlong bean]
These are long beans, generally eaten as a green vegetable. Usually about ¼ inch (0.5 cm) in diameter the bean grows as much as 20 inches (50 cm) long. Generally the ends are trimmed and the beans are cut into short pieces and cooked. This bean provides some protein and dietary fibre as well as potassium and calcium together with Vitamins A and C.

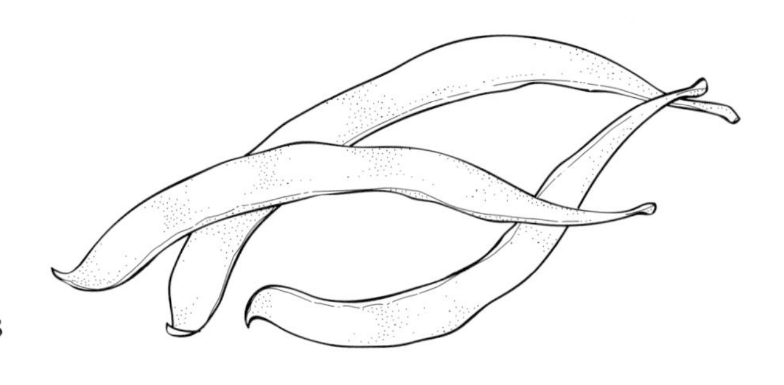

Tomato (*Lycopersicum esculenta*)
Tomatoes are popular both for eating and as a garnish, because of their bright colour and excellent flavour. Though tomatoes have long been popular raw in salads, the cherry tomato and the yellow pear tomato are gaining favour as a cooked side dish, quickly sautéed with herbs. Depending on the variety, the flesh colour can vary from crimson to a brownish purple-pink. The most succulent, flavourful tomatoes are those that are 'vine-ripened', usually only available in speciality produce markets. Unfortunately, such tomatoes are very perishable, which is why supermarkets almost always carry tomatoes that have been picked green

and ripened. Such tomatoes will never have the texture, aroma and taste of the vine-ripened fruit. Choose firm, well-shaped tomatoes that are noticeably fragrant and richly coloured. Unripe fruit can be ripened by placing it in a pierced paper bag with an apple for several days at room temperature (65–75°F/18–25°C). Tomato skins can be removed by blanching.

Tomatoes are rich in Vitamin C and contain appreciable amounts of Vitamins A and B, potassium, iron and phosphorus. A medium tomato has about as much fibre as a slice of wholewheat bread and only about 35 calories.

Peas and beans

Peas and beans are full of nutrients and are often considered the most nutritious foods per calorie. They are also the best sources of fibre available per ounce. They contain hefty amounts of anaemia-fighting iron and the nerve-soothing B vitamins. Eat with Vitamin C-rich foods to boost iron absorption, and with rice or wheat to form complete proteins. Most peas and beans are low in fat and rich in folate. They help to lower your blood-cholesterol levels. To improve the digestibility of beans, soak them in cold water for at least 1 hour, pour away the water and cook as usual.

Pigeon peas (*Cajanus cajan*) [cajanus, gandures, gungo peas, no-eye peas]
These are a favourite in many countries but especially in Barbados, where they are used in every possible dish. It is the main ingredient in their favourite Christmas dish called 'jug'.

Black-eye peas (*Vigna unguiculata*)
Dry black-eye peas are distinctive dry beans from the 'cowpea' family. Scientifically they are peas and not beans, so cause only a negligible amount of flatulence. Further, unlike most beans, they do not require presoaking. Black-eyes are very popular and are thought to have come from Africa, possibly brought by the slaves. They are delicious fresh or dry, but generally are more widely available in the dry form. Among legumes, black-eye peas rank among the highest in protein, and in fact they are the best vegetable source of folate, a B-complex vitamin that is important because it helps to prevent some birth defects, and also allows other water-soluble B-complex vitamins to perform at peak efficiency. They are also a very high source of potassium.

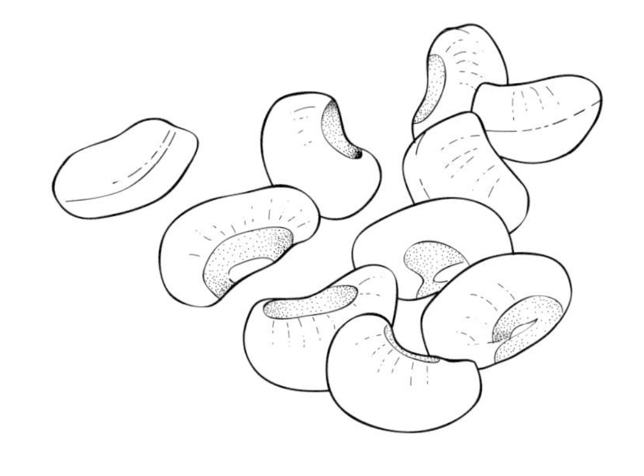

Starchy fruits, roots and tubers

The popular foods within this group are breadfruit, cassava, plantains, green bananas and sweet potatoes.

Breadfruit (*Artocarpus altilis*)
[Captain Bligh, pain bois]
This is a round or oval starchy fruit, which has a rough green skin, pale yellow flesh and a tough centre containing tiny black seeds. This is a versatile fruit which is eaten as a vegetable and can be prepared in a variety of ways, including being processed into flour. Although it is mainly eaten green, the ripe breadfruit can be used in the preparation of some sweet dishes, as the flesh is quite sweet when ripe. The breadfruit is an excellent source of potassium, carbohydrate and fibre.

Cassava (*Manihot esculenta*) [camioc, manioc]
Cassava is a starchy root which is covered by two layers of skin. It is usually peeled and cooked as any other starchy food. When thinly sliced and deep fried it makes delicious crisp chips. There are many varieties of cassava but only two main categories, sweet and bitter. The bitter cassava contains the poisonous prussic acid, which becomes harmless when cooked. Grated, sun-dried cassava is called **cassava meal** or '**conguintay**'. Cassava is also used to make casareep and tapioca. Cassava primarily provides starch, but fresh-cooked cassava is a good source of the antioxidant beta carotene and also of potassium, which can keep blood pressure within normal limits. Cassava also contains bone-building calcium.

Plantain (*Musa paradisiaca*)
[Dominican, hart]
The plantain is one of the most important fruits of the tropics and is used as a vegetable because it is unpalatable when raw. An average plantain weighs approximately 10 oz (284 g). If the plantain is too green when purchased it will wither, without maturing properly. The peel can turn completely black

without affecting quality and it can be used just before it becomes over ripe. There is no set rule, only experience can teach when a plantain is ready for each of its many uses. The best way to store plantains is to hang one or more bunches in a cool, shady place, with the stalk if possible, so that the fruit can continue to receive nutrients. Plantain is generally used as any starchy food and may be used to make chips (crisps), which are a popular snack. Plantain is a good source of carbohydrates and contains significant amounts of potassium.

Sweet potato (*Ipomoea butatas*)
There are several varieties of this vegetable, a herbaceous climber, depending on the climate. Sweet potatoes range in colour from cream to yellow through mauve and pink to deep orange and have varying degrees of sweetness. The leaves, though of a general pattern, vary considerably in shape. The orange/yellow varieties are rich in carotene. Sweet potatoes provide Vitamin A and minerals.

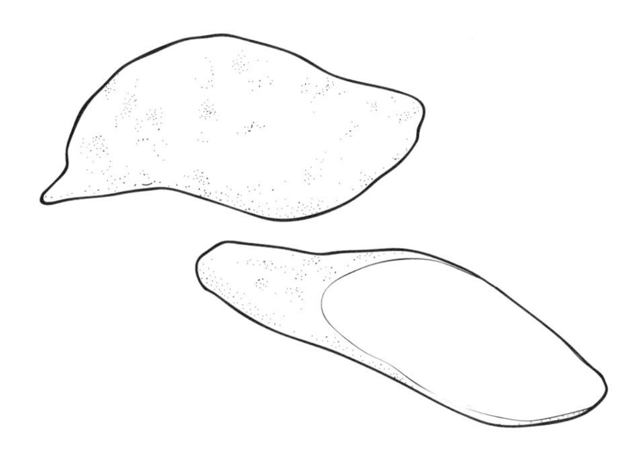

Exotic foods

The Caribbean boasts of two exotic foods which, although technically fruits, are used as vegetables.

Ackee (*Blighia sapida*)
Ackee, the national fruit of Jamaica, has its name derived from the West African 'akye fufo'. Borne in clusters on an evergreen tree, the fruit turns red on reaching maturity and splits open with continued exposure to the sun. Traditionally it is at this time that the ackees are harvested and the arilli removed and cleaned in preparation for cooking. This delicacy is enjoyed by many at breakfast or as an entrée. The canned product is exported to ethnic markets worldwide and continues to be enjoyed by those who have visited the island and Jamaicans residing overseas.

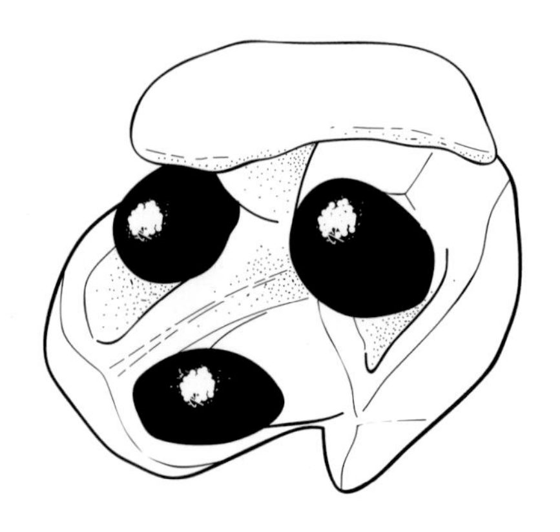

Consumers of the unripe fruit sometimes suffer from 'Jamaican vomiting sickness syndrome' (JVS), allegedly caused by the unusual amino acid components, hypoglycin A and B. Levels of hypoglycin A in the ackee arilli peak at maturity but rapidly diminish to non-detectable levels in the opened fruit, making it safe for consumption. It is important that consumers realize that only the ripe ackees should be eaten. The ackee is high in fat (15.2 g) although it has no cholesterol. It is also a source of calcium, iron, potassium and sodium, together with minimal amounts of the B vitamins.

Breadnut (*Artocarpus altilis 'Seminifera'*) [catahar, chataigne, katahar]
Of all the fruits grown in the Caribbean region, none is as under utilized as the breadnut; yet it is so versatile that many interesting and attractive dishes can be prepared from it. Technically a seeded variety of the breadfruit, breadnut is a round, yellow-green fruit that has short, dull regular spikes covering the skin. Inside, the white nuts covered by brown shells are surrounded by white pulp which may be eaten as it is – shredded like cabbage – or cut into small segments and boiled. It can be curried, or cooked in tomato sauce, and can be substituted for many starchy vegetables. Its function in the preparation of meals for vegetarians is worth mentioning, since it contains a greater amount of protein than other starchy vegetables. Breadnut is regarded as an Indian delicacy and is quite commonly used by Rastafarians. It is a good source of carbohydrate, fibre and protein.

The fruit bowl

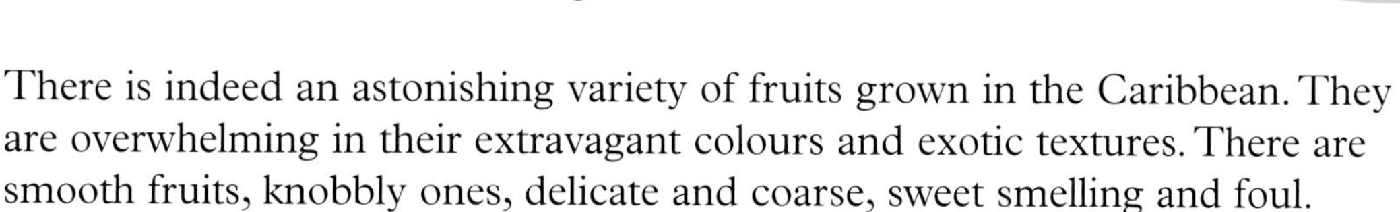

There is indeed an astonishing variety of fruits grown in the Caribbean. They are overwhelming in their extravagant colours and exotic textures. There are smooth fruits, knobbly ones, delicate and coarse, sweet smelling and foul.

Fruits are said to have been grown and eaten by the Indians who lived in the Caribbean Islands long before the voyages of Columbus: in fact the avocado, cashew, soursop, mammee, papaw, guava and pineapple were unknown to Europeans before the islands were discovered.

This bowl of fruits comprises mainly those which have been used in the recipes. However, a few succulent extras have managed to leave their bright colour and exciting aroma among the others. ENJOY…

Avocado (*Persea americana*) [alligator pear, avocat, zaboca, zobooka]
This is a fruit which may be eaten as such or as a vegetable. Sometimes called the avocado pear, because of its shape, this fruit can also be oval or round. The skin is thick, with the colour varying from green to brownish when ripe. The flesh is yellowish green and has a creamy texture when ripe. It is very high in fibre, potassium and magnesium and provides Vitamins A and E and some iron. Exceptionally high in fat (89%), the avocado may be used as an hors d'oeuvre and in salads.

Banana (*Musa sapientum*)
There are many varieties throughout the Caribbean. Due to its high nutritional value and creamy taste, the banana is a preferred food for babies and young children. The green fruit makes a fine, aromatic flour, superior to all others. Bananas are slightly sweet, very nutritious, and easily digested. Ripe bananas should be peeled and eaten immediately because oxidation quickly turns them black. When buying, look for yellow fruit

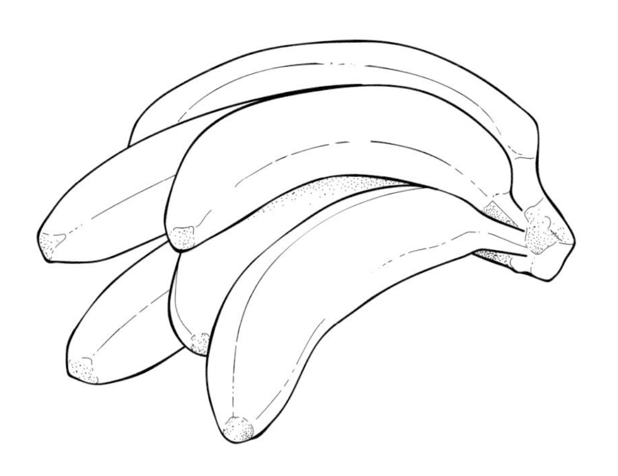

that is slightly green at the ends, firm but not hard. They will ripen in a couple of days. The fruit is primarily composed of water, carbohydrates and a certain amount of protein and fat. Banana is also very rich in magnesium, sodium, potassium, phosphorus and nitrogen. Green bananas contain more starch and less sugar than the ripened fruit.

Carambola/fivefinger (*Averrhoa carambola*) [Chinese star apple, coolie, pommer canelle, star fruit]
This smooth-skinned fruit grows with five lengthwise ridges, and when sliced crosswise each slice is shaped like a star. When ripe, the skin is yellow and the pulp creamy, with a core containing small seeds. It may be eaten raw, made into juice or dried. Stewed sliced carambola may be served as part of a dessert. It makes an attractive design if placed in the bottom of a cake pan instead of pineapple when baking an upside down cake. Carambola is a fair source of Vitamin C, potassium and fibre.

Cashew/ugli (*Anacardium occidentale*) [cajugaha, cashew apple]
This small kidney-shaped fruit is usually red when ripe. It has a good flavour and may be eaten raw but because of the strings inside, it is often better appreciated made into juice or jelly. One ash-grey kidney-shaped nut grows on the bottom of each fruit. It contains an acid juice and a noxious property which is destroyed by roasting. The roasted cashew nut is considered a great delicacy. The cashew fruit is a good source of Vitamins A and C and of fibre. The cashew nut is a good source of protein and fat.

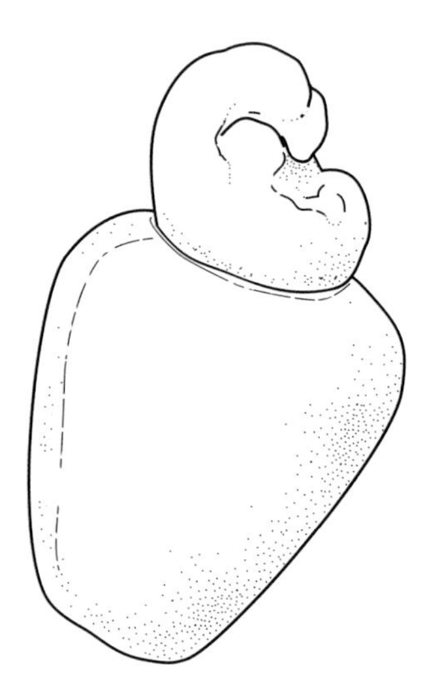

Citrus fruits (*Citrus spp.*)
Orange, lime, lemon, portugal, tangerine, grapefruit, shaddock
These came originally from south-eastern Asia and India. In the early period of agricultural development, crossbreeding of various species was used to

develop several hybrids. A fresh orange or grapefruit can be sectioned and eaten, or squeezed for its juice. Generally, the fruits are rich in potassium, sodium, phosphorus, Vitamin A and, more particularly, Vitamin C. They also contain fibre, which is important in the process of digestion and as a cleanser of the system.

Portugals

Coconut (*Cocos nucifera*) [coco palm]
The green unripe coconut provides a refreshing nutritious drink straight from the shell and is usually sold for its coconut water. When cracked open, a white jelly is revealed and this may be eaten with a spoon. The brown ripe coconut contains the white meat of the mature nut. It may be removed from the shell in pieces and eaten or grated and made into coconut milk, which is used in a variety of ways. The shell may be used as a serving dish for both food and beverage. Coconut has a high fat content and is rich in carbohydrates and minerals. The jelly of the young coconut contains a high percentage of sodium and potassium.

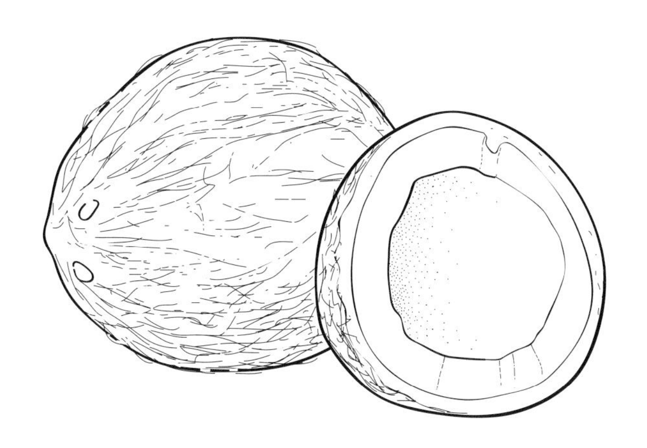

Coco plum (*Chrysobalanus icaco*) [fat pork]
This globe-shaped drupe has a thin pinkish purple skin and a white inner pulp, which is used to make wines and jam and may also be eaten raw. It is a fair source of fibre and Vitamin C.

Golden apple (*Spondias cytherea*) [Jew plum, June plum, pomme cythere]
This fruit is approximately 3 inches

(7.5 cm) long and oval in shape. It may be eaten while the skin is still green and the flesh firm or when it begins to turn yellow and soft. There is a large seed in the centre of the fruit with spines all around. It is generally eaten raw or made into juices, jam, jelly or sauce. It is a good source of Vitamins A and C, and of fibre.

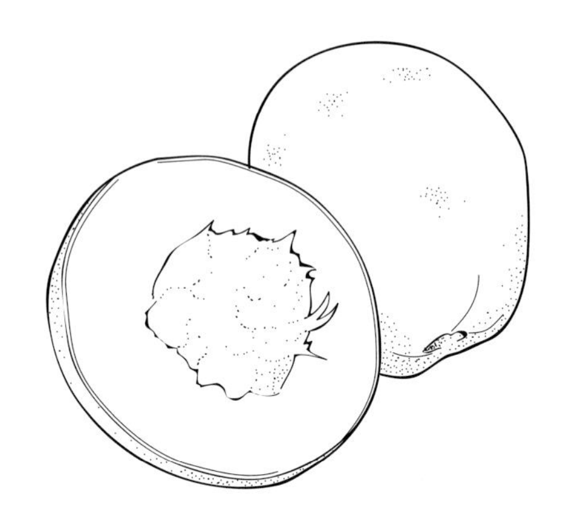

Guava (*Psidium guajava*) [apple guava, yellow guava]
This yellow smooth-skinned fruit has either white or pink pulp with many tiny seeds. It may be eaten raw or stewed, or made into juice, jelly or cheese. The white variety has a better flavour and is less acid. Guavas provide a good source of carbohydrates. They are also an excellent source of Vitamin C and fibre, generally providing two to three times more Vitamin C than orange juice.

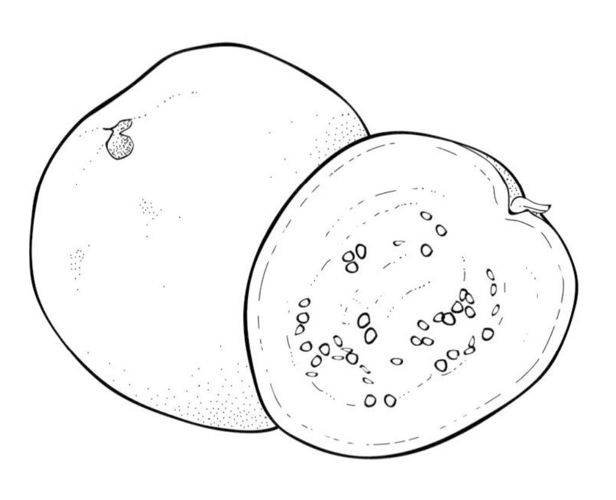

Mammee apple (*Mammea americana*) [abricot, mamey apple, mammee, mammy apple, San Domingo or South American apricot, zaboucaud]
This is a fruit which is globular or oblate in form with a short thick stem. It has a more or less visible floral remnant at the apex. The skin is usually rough and russet brown to greyish brown, while the flesh is light or golden yellow to dark orange. The flesh is not fibrous and can be crispy or juicy, firm or tender, and generally smells pleasant and appetizing. When unripe, the fruit is hard and heavy but it slightly softens when fully ripe. The flesh may be eaten raw or can be preserved and used in confectionery. It is believed that if the mammee apple is eaten with alcohol it can be poisonous. The fruit is very high in fibre and Vitamins A and C.

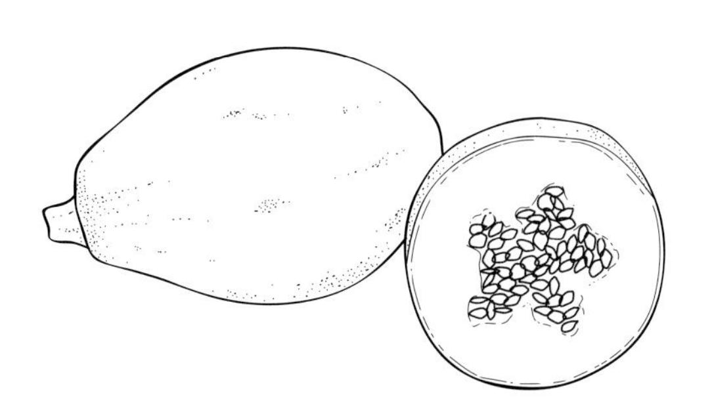

Papaw (*Carica papaya*) [papaya, papayl, popoy, tree melon]
The papaw varies in shape from round to oval, and has a green skin which lightens then becomes orange as the fruit ripens. The ripe flesh is orange to red in colour and most often has several tiny black seeds in the centre. Ripe papaw is good as a fruit eaten alone. The green fruit may be used to prepare chutneys and other preserves, as well as a vegetable and cooked with meat. Both the leaves and the fruit contain papain, which is a protein-digesting enzyme. This is sometimes used to tenderize tough cuts of meat.

Pineapple (*Ananas comosus*) [pine]
This spiky, prickly green and orange-skinned fruit has a pale yellow juicy pulp. The pleasant flavour of the pineapple makes it an excellent appetizer eaten raw. Pineapple is often used in salads, and as juices, sauces and jams. It accompanies poultry and pork dishes for which it must be precooked, since it contains the enzyme bromelin. It may be used in the preparation of cakes, pies and pancakes. Ripe pineapple contains a high percentage of sugar. It is a fair source of vitamins.

Tamarind (*Tamarindus indica*)
It is noteworthy that this fruit is a member of the legume family. It consists of brown-grey pods that contain dark brown edible meat around black seeds. The pulp is used to make sweets, beverages and preserves. The green fruit is very acidic and is often used for flavouring meats and fish.

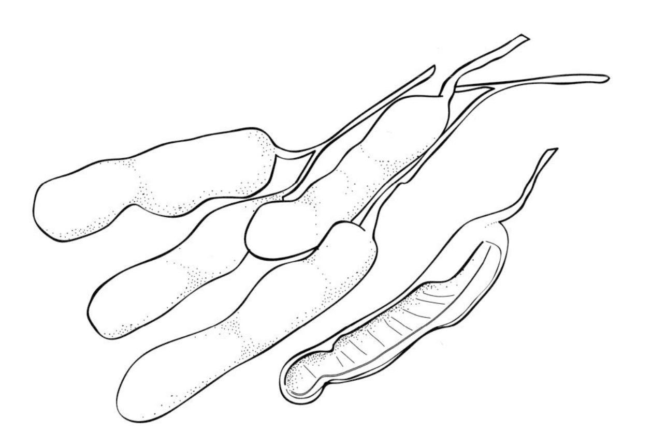

Watermelon (*Citrullus vulgaris*)
There are three basic types of watermelon. There are the spherical ones, among which the most outstanding are 'Sugar Baby', a relatively small melon with a dark green rind and very sweet red meat; 'Black Diamond', which can weigh up to 44 lb (20 kg); and 'Mijako', which has a pale green-striped rind. Then come the huge oval-shaped spotted melons like the 'Charleston Gray', 'Klondike Striped' and 'Dixie Queen'; and lastly, the smaller oval melons that weigh between 11 and 13 lb (5 and 6 kg), such as 'Sweetmeat', a very fragrant and sweet fruit especially appreciated because it is almost seedless.

The colour of the pulp is generally red, although, according to the species, it can have several hues. In the past, yellow-meat watermelons were cultivated. The quite numerous seeds are dark, blackish, spotted or completely black. Watermelon is excellent for quenching thirst and its delicately flavoured juice, lightly chilled, does not require further sweetening. It is also very good in fruit salads. The rind makes a wonderful pickle. The watermelon is almost 95% water and contains a fair amount of Vitamin A and lycopene.

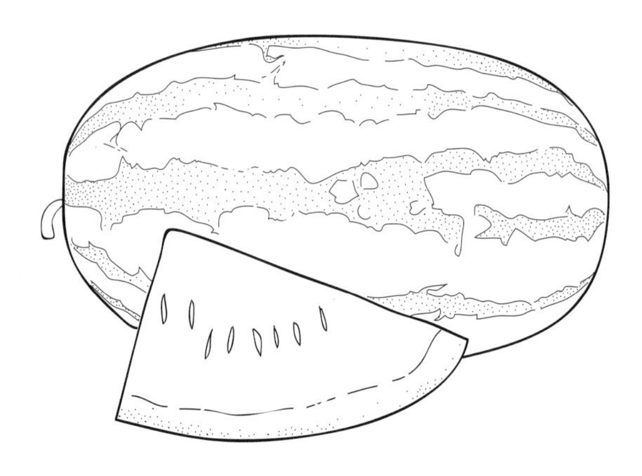

Fruit and vegetable recipes

Apricot cheese
Apricot granola
Apricot liqueur
Avocado choka
Avocado shake
Black-eye punch
Boulanger cakes
Breadfruit surprise
Breadnut pudding
Breadnut punch
Candied breadnut
Candied cashew apple
Carambola achar
Cashew apple chutney
Fat pork jam
Fat pork wine
Ochro leaves, country style
Okracha
Pickled breadnut
Pineapple lamps
Plantain horns
Pumpkin liqueur
Pumpkin nut fudge
Pumpkin wine
Roasted pumpkin seeds
Stuffed baked pumpkin with pumpkin leaves
Sweet and sour apricot

Apricot cheese

(St Lucia)

4 lb (1.8 kg) apricots
about 3¾ lb (1.7 kg) sugar

1. Wash the apricots, peel and remove rag (stringy parts).
2. Cut the flesh from the seeds and weigh the fruit.
3. Cut into medium-sized pieces and purée in ½ pint (280 ml) water.
4. Place the puréed apricot and an equal weight of sugar (about 3 lb/1.4 kg) into a heavy metal saucepan over the heat.
5. Stir constantly to dissolve the sugar.
6. Bring the mixture to the boil, stirring occasionally as the mixture thickens.
7. When it is thick and leaves the sides of the pan, pour into a shallow greased baking pan and allow the cheese to cool.
8. Cut into desired shapes and dust with granulated sugar.

Makes: 49 pieces

Nutrition information

	Per recipe	***Per serving***
Kilocalories	157.7 kcal	3.22 kcal
Protein	0.361 g	0.01 g
Carbohydrate	40.8 g	0.83 g
Fat	0.044 g	0.001 g
Cholesterol	0 mg	0 mg
Dietary fibre	0.889 g	0.02 g
Sodium	1.497 mg	0.03 mg
Iron	0.484 mg	0.01 mg

Apricot granola

(St Lucia)

1 lb (454 g) grated coconut
1 lb (454 g) mixed unsalted nuts
4 oz (113 g) rolled oats
4 tbsp vegetable oil
¼ pint (140 ml) apricot syrup
1 tsp vanilla essence
½ tsp salt
6 oz (168 g) dried candied apricot

1. Place the coconut in a large bowl and add the nuts and oats. Mix thoroughly.
2. Put the oil, syrup, vanilla essence and salt into a saucepan and heat gently until thoroughly mixed.
3. Gradually pour the liquid over the oats mixture and stir in the dried candied apricot.
4. Place the mixture in a shallow baking pan and bake at 350°F for 30 minutes.
5. Remove the pan from oven and stir the granola. Replace in oven.
6. Stir occasionally.
7. When the granola is light brown, remove from the oven and leave to cool.

Serves: 12

Once cooled, the granola will be crunchy.
Stirring occasionally prevents the granola from over browning.

Nutrition information

	Per recipe	***Per serving***
Kilocalories	296.8 kcal	24.73 kcal
Protein	4.774 g	0.39 g
Carbohydrate	28.45 g	2.37 g
Fat	19.57 g	1.63 g
Cholesterol	0 mg	0 mg
Dietary fibre	3.155 g	0.26 g
Sodium	135.7 mg	11.30 mg
Iron	1.843 mg	0.15 mg

Apricot granola (page 119)

Apricot liqueur

(St Lucia)

1½ lb (681 g) granulated sugar
¼ oz (7 g) cinnamon sticks
1 lb (454 g) fresh apricot chunks
½ pint (280 ml) white rum

1. Dissolve the sugar in 2 pints (1.1 litres) water in a heavy aluminium or stainless steel pan.
2. Tie the cinnamon sticks in muslin and add to the sugar solution.
3. Boil to a medium thick syrup which flows slowly off the spoon.
4. Leave the syrup to cool.
5. Blanch the apricots for 3 minutes and place in sterilized jars.
6. Pour the cooled syrup over the apricot chunks.
7. Add the rum and leave for 2 weeks.
8. Strain and pour into sterilized bottles.

Makes: 14 fl oz (400 ml)
Serves: 4

Nutrition information

	Per recipe	*Per serving*
Kilocalories	563.9 kcal	140.9 kcal
Protein	1.104 g	0.28 g
Carbohydrate	122.8 g	30.7 g
Fat	0.331 g	0.08 g
Cholesterol	0 mg	0 mg
Dietary fibre	1.435 g	0.36 g
Sodium	10.16 mg	2.54 mg
Iron	0.98 mg	0.24 mg

Avocado choka

(Guyana)

1 ripe avocado
1 garlic clove
1 onion
½ tsp black pepper
½ tsp pepper sauce
salt or any desired spice to taste

1. Halve avocado and remove seed.
2. Scoop out the flesh of the avocado and purée or crush.
3. Grate the garlic and onion.
4. Mix all the ingredients thoroughly in a bowl. Place on a serving dish.

Serves: 2

Serve with one of the following: cassava bread, fried plantains, bakes or roti.

Nutrition information

	Per recipe	*Per serving*
Kilocalories	313.1 kcal	156.55 kcal
Protein	5.58 g	2.79 g
Carbohydrate	10.3 g	5.15 g
Fat	31.11 g	15.56 g
Cholesterol	0 mg	0 mg
Dietary fibre	26.28 g	13.14 g
Sodium	653.1 mg	326.55 mg
Iron	1.67 mg	0.84 mg

Avocado shake

(Guyana)

1 ripe avocado
1 pint (560 ml) milk
1 oz (28 g) sugar
¼ tsp vanilla essence
¼ tsp nutmeg

1. Halve the avocado, remove the seed and scoop out the flesh.
2. Purée or crush and place in a mixing bowl.
3. Add the milk, sugar, vanilla essence and nutmeg.
4. Stir until the mixture is smooth then whisk for a few minutes.
5. Pour into a jug and chill before serving.

Serves: 3

Nutrition information

	Per recipe	*Per serving*
Kilocalories	620.6 kcal	206.9 kcal
Protein	18.36 g	6.12 g
Carbohydrate	51.9 g	17.3 g
Fat	38.18 g	12.73 g
Cholesterol	66 mg	22 mg
Dietary fibre	6.572 g	2.19 g
Sodium	249.6 mg	83.2 mg
Iron	2.89 mg	0.96 mg

Black-eye punch

(Guyana)

4 oz (113 g) boiled black-eye peas
3 tbsp brown sugar
4 oz (113 g) powdered milk
½ pint (280 ml) water
¼ tsp nutmeg

Blend together all the ingredients until smooth and serve cold.

Makes: 14 fl oz (400 ml)
Serves: 4

Nutrition information

	Per recipe	*Per serving*
Kilocalories	901.2 kcal	225.3 kcal
Protein	44.49 g	11.12 g
Carbohydrate	111.8 g	27.95 g
Fat	31.89 g	7.98 g
Cholesterol	15.27 mg	3.82 mg
Dietary fibre	15.8 g	3.95 g
Sodium	366.8 mg	91.7 mg
Iron	4.88 mg	1.22 mg

Boulanger cakes

(Guyana)

2 large boulangers (eggplants)
6 oz (168 g) dried breadcrumbs or biscuit crumbs
2 tbsp chopped eschallot and celery
2 eggs
1 tbsp margarine
oil for frying

To garnish:
chopped parsley or celery
chopped red sweet pepper

1. Roast the boulangers.
2. Remove the skin and mash.
3. Add two thirds of the crumbs, the eschallot and celery, and salt and pepper to taste to the mashed boulanger.
4. Beat 1 egg.
5. Add margarine to the mixture and sufficient beaten egg to bind together. Shape the mixture into cakes.
6. Beat the remaining egg and use to coat the cakes together with the remaining dried crumbs.
7. Fry in shallow fat (oil) and drain well.
8. Garnish with parsley or celery and chopped sweet pepper.

Makes: 10

Nutrition information

	Per recipe	*Per serving*
Kilocalories	1432 kcal	143.2 kcal
Protein	31.43 g	3.14 g
Carbohydrate	154.2 g	15.42 g
Fat	79.12 g	7.91 g
Cholesterol	342 mg	34.2 mg
Dietary fibre	1.811 g	0.18 g
Sodium	2248 mg	224.8mg
Iron	12.89mg	1.29 mg

Breadfruit

Breadfruit surprise

(Guyana)

8 oz (227 g) ripe breadfruit
1 pint (560 ml) milk
4 oz (113 g) sugar
⅛ tsp nutmeg
½ tsp vanilla essence

1. Boil the breadfruit and crush smoothly.
2. Blend all the remaining ingredients with the crushed breadfruit until thick and creamy.
3. Serve chilled breadfruit surprise as a delicious dessert.

Serves: 3

Nutrition information

	Per recipe	*Per serving*
Kilocalories	991.5 kcal	330.5 kcal
Protein	18.05 g	6.02 g
Carbohydrate	174.4 g	58.13 g
Fat	17.51 g	5.84 g
Cholesterol	66 mg	22 mg
Dietary fibre	0 g	0 g
Sodium	629.6 mg	209.9 mg
Iron	5.42 mg	1.81 mg

Breadnut pudding

(St Lucia)

4 oz (113 g) margarine
8 oz (227 g) sugar
1 egg
4 tbsp skimmed milk powder
1½ lb (681 g) breadnuts, grated
2 tsp baking powder
1 tsp molasses
1½ tsp nutmeg
1 tsp grated orange rind
2 tsp vanilla essence
2 tsp salt
4 tbsp milk or water

1. Cream the margarine and sugar until light and fluffy.
2. Add the egg and beat well.
3. In another bowl, blend the powdered milk into the grated breadnut.
4. Gradually fold the breadnut mixture into the egg mixture.
5. Incorporate the baking powder and the molasses, nutmeg, orange rind, vanilla and salt.
6. Add enough milk or water to mix to a light dropping consistency.
7. Spread the mixture into a 6-inch (15-cm) round greased baking pan.
8. Bake at 375°F for 50 minutes or until lightly brown and well done.
9. Allow the pudding to stand in the pan for about 5 minutes.
10. Serve warm or cold.

Serves: 12

Nutrition information

	Per recipe	*Per serving*
Kilocalories	2350 kcal	195.8 kcal
Protein	18.89 g	1.57 g
Carbohydrate	350.1 g	29.18 g
Fat	99.8 g	8.32 g
Cholesterol	215.2 mg	17.93 mg
Dietary fibre	0.204 g	0.02 g
Sodium	5585 mg	465.4 mg
Iron	28.02 mg	2.34 mg

Breadnut punch

(St Lucia)

12 oz (340 g) boiled shelled breadnuts
½ pint (280 ml) milk
4 tbsp evaporated milk
8 oz (227 g) sugar
⅛ tsp salt
1 tbsp rum or brandy
¼ tsp nutmeg
1 tsp vanilla essence

1. Mash the breadnuts.
2. Add all the other ingredients and blend.
3. Strain and serve with ice cubes.

Serves: 3

Nutrition information

	Per recipe	*Per serving*
Kilocalories	870.7 kcal	290.2 kcal
Protein	14.34 g	4.78 g
Carbohydrate	157.1 g	52.36 g
Fat	14.24 g	4.74 g
Cholesterol	51.28 mg	17.09 mg
Dietary fibre	0 g	0 g
Sodium	842.7 mg	280.9 mg
Iron	5.45 mg	1.81 mg

Breadnut punch (page 129)

Candied breadnut

(St Lucia)

1 lb (454 g) sugar
12 oz (340 g) boiled shelled breadnuts
1 cinnamon stick

1. Make a syrup by combining the sugar with ¼ pint (140 ml) water and boiling over high heat.
2. Add the breadnuts and the cinnamon stick.
3. Continue boiling until the syrup reaches the softball stage.
4. Allow the breadnuts to stand in the syrup overnight.
5. Remove the breadnuts from the syrup and place on a wire rack.
6. Allow to dry in the sun.
7. Keep the candied breadnuts in jars or plastic bags.

Serves: 6

Serve as a dessert or as an accompaniment.
Breadnut in syrup can be made using the same method, but remove from the heat before the syrup gets to the softball stage.

Nutrition information

	Per recipe	***Per serving***
Kilocalories	1876 kcal	312.7 kcal
Protein	1.996 g	0.33 g
Carbohydrate	479.3 g	79.88 g
Fat	1.129 g	0.19 g
Cholesterol	0 mg	0 mg
Dietary fibre	0 g	0 g
Sodium	568.8 mg	94.8 mg
Iron	13.97 mg	2.33 mg

Candied cashew apple

(St Lucia)

3 lb (1.4 kg) sugar
3 lb (1.4 kg) firm steamed cashew fruit
6 cloves

1. Make a syrup by combining the sugar with 1½ pints (840 ml) water and boiling over high heat.
2. Cut the steamed fruit into ½-inch (1-cm) thick slices.
3. Pour the syrup over the fruit, add the cloves and allow to boil over a medium heat.
4. The candied fruit is ready when the syrup thickens and both syrup and fruit are golden brown in colour.
5. Strain the syrup from the fruit and dry the fruit pieces out in the sun on a tray over a period of days. The fruit can also be dried very slowly in an oven.

Serves: 20

The candied fruit can be dipped in water immediately after cooking to remove excess syrup before drying.

It is easier, though it takes longer, to dry the candied fruit in the sun. The fruit has a high moisture content and too much oven heat will soften it further.

Nutrition information

	Per recipe	*Per serving*
Kilocalories	5993.8 kcal	299.69 kcal
Protein	17.7 g	0.89 g
Carbohydrate	1520.5 g	76.03 g
Fat	2.73 g	0.136 g
Cholesterol	0 mg	0 mg
Dietary fibre	18.43 g	0.93 g
Sodium	81.72 mg	4.86 mg
Iron	25.88 mg	1.294 mg

Carambola achar

(Guyana)

2 lb (908 g) carambolas, just under-ripe
1 tbsp gheera (cumin)
1 tbsp garam masala
1 tbsp mangrile
1 onion
6 garlic cloves
8 wiri-wiri peppers
1 tbsp cooking oil

1. Wash and slice the fruits.
2. Squeeze the fruits to remove some of the juice.
3. Parch and grind the gheera, garam masala and mangrile.
4. Chop the onion, garlic and peppers very finely.
5. Mix all ingredients with the carambola.
6. Add enough salt to taste.
7. Heat the oil in a heavy pan and add the carambola mixture.
8. Cook until the liquid from the carambola dries out.
9. Fry for another 3 minutes.
10. Pour into sterilized bottles.

Serves: 24

Nutrition information

	Per recipe	***Per serving***
Kilocalories	443.6 kcal	18.48 kcal
Protein	10.24 g	0.43 g
Carbohydrate	95.24 g	3.97 g
Fat	6.323 g	0.26 g
Cholesterol	0 mg	0 mg
Dietary fibre	15.03 g	0.63 g
Sodium	575.8 mg	23.99 mg
Iron	5.502 mg	0.23 mg

Cashew apple chutney

(St Lucia)

1 lb (454 g) onions, finely chopped
½ pint (280 ml) vinegar
2 lb (908 g) steamed cashew fruit
4 oz (113 g) dried fruit
1 tsp salt
1 tsp ground ginger
1 tsp pickling spice
12 oz (340 g) sugar

1. Put the onions into a saucepan with 4 tablespoons vinegar and simmer until just tender.
2. Chop the cashew coarsely. Add to the saucepan with the dried fruit, salt, ginger and the pickling spice (tied in muslin), and enough vinegar to stop the mixture from burning.
3. Simmer until the fruit is soft, stirring from time to time.
4. Add the remainder of the vinegar and thoroughly stir in the sugar.
5. Boil steadily until the chutney is thick. Remove the pickling spices.
6. Pour into hot jars and cover.

Makes: 3 x 20-oz (560-g) jars
Serves: 60

This chutney can be eaten straightaway or stored for a while to allow the flavours to develop.

Nutrition information

	Per recipe	*Per serving*
Kilocalories	2125.7 kcal	35.43 kcal
Protein	12.7 g	0.212 g
Carbohydrate	543.64 g	9.06 g
Fat	2.8 g	0.047 g
Cholesterol	0 mg	0 mg
Dietary fibre	16.41 g	0.274 g
Sodium	1960 mg	32.67 mg
Iron	15.78 mg	0.263 mg

Fat pork jam

(Guyana)

1 lb (454 g) fat pork (coco plum)
8 oz (227 g) white sugar
¼ tsp lime juice

1. Wash and remove the skin from the fat pork.
2. Place the fruit in a clean pot and add enough water (about ¼ pint/140 ml) to prevent burning.
3. Cook the fruit slowly.
4. Remove from the heat and pass through a sieve.
5. Add the sugar and lime juice to the sieved pulp.
6. Boil until setting point is reached.
7. Pour into sterilized jars, cover and label.

Serves: 20

Nutrition information

	Per recipe	*Per serving*
Kilocalories	1149 kcal	57.45 kcal
Protein	3.272 g	0.16 g
Carbohydrate	297.5 g	14.88 g
Fat	1.046 g	0.05 g
Cholesterol	0 mg	0 mg
Dietary fibre	6.789 g	0.34 g
Sodium	70.42 mg	3.52 mg
Iron	1.005 mg	0.05 mg

Fat pork wine

(Guyana)

4 lb (1.8 kg) fat pork (coco plum)
4 lb (1.8 kg) sugar
1 tsp active dry yeast

1. Wash the fat pork.
2. Place in a jar with the sugar, yeast and 3 pints (1.8 litres) water.
3. Cover and leave for 6 weeks.
4. Strain the wine and pour into sterilized bottles.

Serves: 32

Nutrition information

	Per recipe	*Per serving*
Kilocalories	7929 kcal	247.8 kcal
Protein	14.6 g	0.46 g
Carbohydrate	2048 g	64 g
Fat	4.364 g	0.14 g
Cholesterol	0 mg	0 mg
Dietary fibre	27.99 g	0.87 g
Sodium	1007 mg	31.47 mg
Iron	38.73 mg	1.21 mg

Ochro leaves, country style

(Antigua)

4 oz (113 g) chopped young ochro leaves
4 oz (113 g) flour
¼ pint (140 ml) water
1 onion, finely chopped
1 egg, beaten
1 tbsp minced sweet pepper
1 tbsp minced celery
a pinch of salt
⅛ tsp black pepper
oil for frying

1. Place the chopped leaves in a mixing bowl.
2. Add the other ingredients and mix well to a dropping consistency.
3. Drop the batter by spoonfuls into hot oil.
4. Fry slowly until golden brown.

Serves: 8

Young ochro leaves are recommended for all recipes as the older ones contain hairs that may irritate the tongue.

Nutrition information

	Per recipe	*Per serving*
Kilocalories	1312 kcal	164 kcal
Protein	26.5 g	3.31 g
Carbohydrate	101.4 g	12.67 g
Fat	91.48 g	11.43 g
Cholesterol	217.5 mg	27.19 mg
Dietary fibre	7.347 g	0.91 g
Sodium	2030 mg	253.7 mg
Iron	9.143mg	1.14 mg

Okracha

(Antigua)

6 eggplants (garden eggs)
8 oz (227 g) pumpkin
4 small ripe tomatoes
8 oz (227 g) salted meat
8 oz (227 g) chicken portions
8 oz (227 g) fresh meat
1 lb (454 g) pigeon peas (gungo peas)
2 small onions, chopped
1 hot pepper
chive, thyme, garlic and cloves (use moderately for flavouring)

1. Wash the eggplant, pumpkin and tomatoes and cut into small pieces.
2. Cut the meat in bite-sized pieces and cook in 2 pints (1.1 litres) salted water.
3. Add the vegetables once the meats are cooked, so that they will not be overcooked.
4. Add all the other ingredients and season with salt and pepper to taste.
5. Cook until the mixture is thick. Serve hot.

Serves: 8

Small dumplings or cooked sweet potatoes can be added before serving.

Nutrition information

	Per recipe	***Per serving***
Kilocalories	319.2 kcal	39.9 kcal
Protein	24.76 g	3.09 g
Carbohydrate	23.19 g	2.89 g
Fat	14.38 g	1.79 g
Cholesterol	79.24 mg	9.90 mg
Dietary fibre	2.043 g	0.25 g
Sodium	637.1 mg	79.63 mg
Iron	3.104 mg	0.38 mg

Pickled breadnut

(St Lucia)

1¼ lb (567 g) boiled shelled breadnuts
4 onion slices
½ pint (280 ml) white vinegar

1. Arrange the boiled breadnuts and onion slices loosely in a glass jar.
2. Heat the vinegar.
3. Pour the hot vinegar over the breadnuts in the jar.
4. Seal the jar.
5. Wipe jar and label when cooled.

Serves: 10

Nutrition information

	Per recipe	*Per serving*
Kilocalories	267.3 kcal	26.73 kcal
Protein	3.425 g	0.34 g
Carbohydrate	59.92 g	5.99 g
Fat	1.731 g	0.17 g
Cholesterol	0 mg	0 mg
Dietary fibre	0.68 g	0.07 g
Sodium	582.9 mg	58.29 mg
Iron	7.743 mg	0.77 mg

Pineapple lamps

(Guyana)

3 pineapple slices, each about 3 inches (7.5 cm) thick
3 ripe firm bananas
2 tbsp pineapple jam
4 oz (113 g) peanuts, finely chopped
3 glacé cherries

1. Remove core from the pineapple slices.
2. Peel the bananas and cut off the curved ends so that the bananas stand quite straight.
3. Roll the bananas in the jam and chopped nuts.
4. Fit each banana into a pineapple ring. Secure with toothpicks.
5. Stick one glacé cherry on top of each banana to make the lamp 'flame'.
6. Cut fine strips from the pineapple rings and curve to make handles for the lamps.
7. Secure the handles with toothpicks.
8. Chill before serving.

Serves: 3

Nutrition information

	Per recipe	***Per serving***
Kilocalories	1461.9 kcal	487.3 kcal
Protein	34.38 g	11.46 g
Carbohydrate	213.78 g	71.26 g
Fat	59.64 g	19.88 g
Cholesterol	0 mg	0 mg
Dietary fibre	28.05 g	9.35 g
Sodium	929.1 mg	309.7 mg
Iron	4.89 mg	1.63 mg

Bananas *(see page 141)*

Plantain horns

(Guyana)

2 large ripe firm plantains
2 oz (56 g) cheese, grated
2 tsp mayonnaise
1 tbsp mixed chopped herbs (eschallot, celery, pepper, onion)
¼ tsp mustard
2 tbsp crushed pineapple (optional)
1 egg, beaten
1 oz (28 g) breadcrumbs for coating
fat for deep frying
chopped celery and wiri-wiri pepper to garnish

1. Peel, wash and cut the plantains in half crosswise.
2. Boil with salt until cooked but not soft. Drain.
3. When cool, scoop out some of the flesh, leaving a case about ¼–⅜ inch (0.5–0.7 cm).
4. Crush the scooped-out flesh finely.
5. Mix with half the grated cheese and all the other ingredients except the egg and breadcrumbs.
6. Coat the plantain cases with beaten egg and a mixture of breadcrumbs and the remaining cheese.
7. Fry in deep fat.
8. When cool fill with the seasoned crushed flesh.
9. Garnish with chopped celery and wiri-wiri pepper.

Makes: 4

Try plantain wheels: cut plantains across into 1-inch (2.5-cm) thick slices and proceed as above.

Nutrition information

	Per recipe	***Per serving***
Kilocalories	1629 kcal	407.25 kcal
Protein	30.13 g	7.53 g
Carbohydrate	190.8 g	47.7 g
Fat	91.18 g	22.79 g
Cholesterol	268.2 mg	67.05 mg
Dietary fibre	12.25 g	3.06 g
Sodium	1548 mg	387 mg
Iron	7.362mg	1.84 mg

Pumpkin liqueur

(Antigua)

2 lb (908 g) pumpkin
1 lb (454 g) sugar
½ pint (280 ml) white rum
¼ pint (140 ml) lime juice

1. Wash and peel the pumpkin and slice into thin slices.
2. Place alternate layers of pumpkin and sugar in a clean plastic or glass container.
3. Cover and leave overnight.
4. Strain off the syrup.
5. Add the rum and lime juice to the syrup and leave for 21 days.
6. Pour into sterilized bottles and allow the liqueur to mature for 3 months.

Serves: 8

The liqueur improves with age.

Nutrition information

	Per recipe	*Per serving*
Kilocalories	2327 kcal	290.87 kcal
Protein	9.612 g	1.20 g
Carbohydrate	470.1 g	58.76 g
Fat	1.061 g	0.13 g
Cholesterol	0 mg	0 mg
Dietary fibre	15.64 g	1.96 g
Sodium	15.05 mg	1.88 mg
Iron	7.775 mg	0.97 mg

Pumpkin nut fudge

(Antigua)

1 oz (28 g) margarine
¼ pint (140 ml) milk
8 oz (227 g) granulated sugar
4 oz (113 g) pumpkin, cooked and mashed
1 tbsp cracked pumpkin seeds
½ tsp vanilla essence

1. Melt the margarine in a saucepan.
2. Add the milk and sugar to the melted margarine.
3. Cook until the mixture forms a soft ball when a small amount is dropped in water.
4. Add the mashed pumpkin and continue to cook until the fudge is thick.
5. Add the cracked pumpkin seeds and vanilla essence and stir.
6. Pour into greased tins and allow the fudge to harden.
7. Cut into squares.

Makes: 16 squares

Nutrition information

	Per recipe	*Per serving*
Kilocalories	1102 kcal	68.88 kcal
Protein	5.894 g	0.37 g
Carbohydrate	214.8 g	13.43 g
Fat	27.82 g	1.74 g
Cholesterol	16.5 mg	1.03 mg
Dietary fibre	5.178 g	0.32 g
Sodium	1.03 mg	0.06 mg
Iron	332.6 mg	20.78 mg

Pumpkin wine

(Antigua)

2 lb (908 g) pumpkin
4 oz (113 g) rice
4 oz (113 g) raisins
2 oranges
3 lb (1.4 kg) sugar
1 oz (28 g) active dry yeast

1. Boil the pumpkin and rice in 12 pints (7 litres) water for 10 minutes.
2. Add the raisins and boil for another 5 minutes.
3. Peel and slice the oranges and add to the mixture.
4. Boil for 1 minute more.
5. Strain. Add the sugar and stir until it is dissolved.
6. Allow to cool, then add the yeast.
7. Cover and store for 9 days.
8. Strain and pour into sterilized bottles.

Makes: 12 x 18-fl oz (500-ml) bottles

Nutrition information

	Per recipe	*Per serving*
Kilocalories	6247 kcal	521 kcal
Protein	58.8 g	4.88 g
Carbohydrate	1564 g	130.33 g
Fat	6.919 g	0.58 g
Cholesterol	0 mg	0 mg
Dietary fibre	59.59 g	4.97 g
Sodium	782 mg	65.16 mg
Iron	54.47 mg	4.54 mg

Roasted pumpkin seeds

(Antigua)

8 oz (227 g) pumpkin seeds
1 tsp salt
¼ pint (140 ml) cooking oil (optional)

1. Clean and wash the pumpkin seeds.
2. Soak the seeds in salted water for 20 minutes.
3. Drain off the water and dry the seeds.
4. Roast the seeds in a greased frying pan on a flame or deep fat fry.
5. Serve hot or cold. Remove shell if desired.

Serves: 6

Nutrition information

	Per recipe	*Per serving*
Kilocalories	285 kcal	47.5 kcal
Protein	11.9 g	1.98 g
Carbohydrate	34.4 g	5.73 g
Fat	12.4 g	2.06 g
Cholesterol	0 mg	0 mg
Dietary fibre	29.4 g	4.9 g
Sodium	1078 mg	179.6 mg
Iron	2.12 mg	0.35 mg

Stuffed baked pumpkin with pumpkin leaves

(Antigua)

1 small pumpkin
1 tsp salt
1 lb (454 g) young pumpkin leaves with stems
1 small onion
1 tbsp margarine
4 tbsp cooking oil
12 oz (340 g) salted fish, soaked and flaked
1 small tomato, chopped
4 oz (113 g) cheese, grated
4 oz (113 g) dried breadcrumbs
1 green sweet pepper, chopped, to garnish

1. Wash the pumpkin and remove a small portion at the stem.
2. Scoop out the seeds and fibres.
3. Cook the pumpkin in salted water until tender. Take care not to overcook.
4. Scoop out the pumpkin flesh from the shell, being careful not to damage the shell.
5. Wash the pumpkin leaves thoroughly. Remove the stalks and discard. Cut into small pieces.
6. Slice the onion. Sauté the onion in the margarine and add the leaves. Cover and cook until tender.
7. Heat the oil and fry the salted fish with the chopped tomato. Add to the pumpkin leaves.
8. Spoon the pumpkin leaves and salted fish into the cooked pumpkin shell.
9. Sprinkle the top with the grated cheese and breadcrumbs. Bake in a moderate oven (350°F) until lightly brown. Serve hot, garnished with chopped green pepper.

Serves: 4

Nutrition information

	Per recipe	*Per serving*
Kilocalories	498.3 kcal	124.57 kcal
Protein	36.29 g	9.07 g
Carbohydrate	30.63 g	7.66 g
Fat	27.81 g	6.95 g
Cholesterol	74.32 mg	18.58 mg
Dietary fibre	9.577 g	2.39 g
Sodium	1074 mg	268.5 mg
Iron	5.234mg	1.33 mg

Sweet and sour apricot

(St Lucia)

12 fl oz (420 ml) wine vinegar
10 oz (283 g) sugar
1 cinnamon stick
1 lb (454 g) firm ripe apricots

1. Pour the vinegar into a stainless steel pan.
2. Warm on a low heat, then add the sugar.
3. Stir until the sugar is completely dissolved.
4. Add the cinnamon stick to the mixture and allow it to boil until it reaches the consistency of light syrup.
5. Wash the apricots. Peel neatly and cut the flesh into thick slices.
6. Arrange the slices neatly in sterilized jars.
7. Pour the boiling mixture over the fruit to cover it completely. Seal tightly.
8. Allow the preserve to stand for 2–3 months before serving.

Serves: 6

Serve the preserve with roasted or baked meats or with ham.
Dried fruits (raisins, currants) may be added to the apricots.

Nutrition information

	Per recipe	***Per serving***
Kilocalories	1287 kcal	214.5 kcal
Protein	6.393 g	1.07 g
Carbohydrate	327.2 g	54.53 g
Fat	1.808 g	0.30 g
Cholesterol	0 mg	0 mg
Dietary fibre	8.609 g	1.43 g
Sodium	115.7mg	19.28 mg
Iron	8.294 mg	1.38 mg

Main dishes

Beans in yellow boats
Calypso peas
Chicken yammays
Crunchy balls
Farine pie
Fish coubouillon
Pigeon peas pinwheel
Salt fish and vegetables in rice ball
Shrimperi loaf
Sweet salt fish cakes
Vegetarian roll
Zesty legume loaf

Beans in yellow boats

(Guyana)

2 large firm yellow plantains
4 oz (113 g) boiled beans
4 oz (113 g) cooked meat or fish, minced
2 tbsp chopped herbs
2 oz (56 g) margarine
4 oz (113 g) cheese, grated

1. Cut the plantains in half, lengthwise, reserving the skins to make the plantain cases.
2. Boil the plantains until soft and mash.
3. Combine the beans and minced meat or fish with the plantain.
4. Season the mixture with the chopped herbs and salt and pepper. Add the margarine.
5. Fill the plantain cases with the mixture. Sprinkle with the grated cheese.
6. Fix with a skewer or toothpick in order to keep a good shape. Place the filled cases on a baking sheet.
7. Bake in a hot oven (400°F) for 10 minutes or grill for 2 minutes.

Serves: 4

Nutrition information

	Per recipe	*Per serving*
Kilocalories	1708 kcal	427 kcal
Protein	59.06 g	14.77 g
Carbohydrate	194.4 g	48.6 g
Fat	81 g	20.25 g
Cholesterol	173.2 mg	43.3 mg
Dietary fibre	18.1 g	4.5 g
Sodium	2652 mg	663 mg
Iron	6.864 mg	1.716 mg

Calypso peas (page 154)

Calypso peas

(Guyana)

3 oz (84 g) black-eye peas
3 oz (84 g) pigeon peas
3 oz (84 g) red peas
4 oz (113 g) carrots
1 small bundle of bora (string beans)
2 sweet peppers
3 oz (84 g) sweetcorn kernels
2 tbsp cooking oil
2 tbsp margarine
2 small onions, finely chopped
1 tbsp finely chopped celery
2 small wiri-wiri peppers, chopped
1½ tsp salt

1. Soak the peas for about 3 hours or overnight.
2. Drain and place in 1¾ pints (1 litre) boiling water and cook until soft. Do not allow the peas to become mashed. Remove the peas from the liquid.
3. Grate or dice the carrots. Cut the bora into ¼-inch (0.5-cm) lengths. Cut the sweet peppers into rings or 1-inch (2.5-cm) strips. Drain the liquid from the corn.
4. Heat the oil and margarine together. Add the chopped onion, celery and peppers and sauté for about 2 minutes. Add the prepared vegetables and cook for another 2 minutes.
5. Add the peas and stir-fry for about 2 minutes. Season with the salt. Remove from the heat.
6. Pile into a serving dish and garnish with chopped sweet pepper, if wished. Serve hot.

Serves: 4

Any combination of pulses (dried peas) may be used.

Nutrition information

	Per recipe	***Per serving***
Kilocalories	955.6 kcal	238.9 kcal
Protein	23.664 g	5.916 g
Carbohydrate	107 g	26.75 g
Fat	52.28 g	13.07 g
Cholesterol	0 mg	0 mg
Dietary fibre	18.468 g	4.617 g
Sodium	3576 mg	894 mg
Iron	6.644 mg	1.661 mg

Chicken yammays

(Barbados)

1½ lb (681 g) chicken breasts
2 tbsp chicken fat
2 tbsp grated onion
½ tsp white pepper
1 tsp salt
1¼ lb (570 g) raw yam, grated
2 heaped tbsp each finely shredded carrots, spinach and beet
6 sections of singed banana leaf, each 10 x 12 inches (25 x 30 cm)

For the marinade:
2 shelled 5-inch (12.5-cm) tamarinds
½ tsp white pepper
½ tsp ground ginger
½ tsp cinnamon
1 garlic clove, finely chopped
2 tbsp grated onion
2 tsp salt

1. Remove tamarind seeds and mix all ingredients for the marinade.
2. Remove fat from chicken. Cut into small pieces and rub with the marinade.
3. Leave overnight in refrigerator or at room temperature for at least 2 hours.
4. Heat the chicken fat in a pan. Add the chicken and stir-fry.
5. Cover and leave to simmer for 5 minutes or until cooked. Mince coarsely.
6. Add the onion, pepper and salt to the yam. Mix well and divide into three portions. To each portion add a different shredded vegetable.
7. Divide each portion into two and spread on banana leaves.
8. Divide chicken into six portions and heap one on top of each yam portion.
9. Fold over each leaf to make a neat package. Tie securely with cotton thread and steam for approximately 30 minutes.
10. Unwrap and serve hot with butter sauce, or leave wrapped and serve cold as finger food.

Serves: 6

Nutrition information

	Per recipe	*Per serving*
Kilocalories	2201 kcal	366.83 kcal
Protein	196.9 g	32.8 g
Carbohydrate	171.2 g	28.5 g
Fat	77.1 g	12.9 g
Cholesterol	535.4 mg	89.2 mg
Dietary fibre	16.16 g	2.69 g
Sodium	6896 mg	1149 mg
Iron	10.84 mg	1.81 mg

Chicken yammays (page 155)

Crunchy balls

(Guyana)

8 oz (227 g) beans, presoaked and minced
8 oz (227 g) parched peanuts, chopped
1 oz (28 g) margarine
2 tbsp chopped herbs
½ tsp salt
1 egg, beaten
½ pint (280 ml) oil

To garnish:
½ tsp chopped wiri-wiri pepper
½ tsp chopped parsley

1. Combine the minced beans with the peanuts, margarine, chopped herbs, salt and a little pepper.
2. Bind the mixture with beaten egg. Shape into eight balls.
3. Deep fry in the oil and drain.
4. Garnish with the wiri-wiri pepper and parsley.
5. Serve on a platter.

Makes: 8

Make the balls half the size and serve on toothpicks as an appetizer.

Nutrition information

	Per recipe	*Per serving*
Kilocalories	2316 kcal	289.5 kcal
Protein	72.99 g	9.13 g
Carbohydrate	106.2 g	13.3 g
Fat	190.7 g	23.8 g
Cholesterol	0 mg	0 mg
Dietary fibre	31.93 g	3.99 g
Sodium	2649 mg	331 mg
Iron	11.01 mg	1.38 mg

Farine pie

(Guyana)

1 lb (454 g) farine
1 lb (454 g) minced beef or tasso (see below)
1 oz (28 g) herbs, chopped
4 oz (113 g) margarine
4 oz (113 g) peanuts, ground
3 tbsp all-purpose sauce
2 eggs
1 pint (560 ml) milk or stock

1. Soak and drain the farine. Leave for 20 minutes.
2. Season the mince with the chopped herbs and salt and pepper to taste and cook in heated margarine for 5 minutes.
3. Mix the farine and cooked mince in a bowl with all the other ingredients.
4. Spread on a greased pan and bake in a moderate oven, 350°F, until golden brown.

Serves: 8

Tasso is beef which has been cut into strips and sun dried as a means of preservation. It is normally eaten with farine.
Serve this dish with steamed vegetables or a raw vegetable salad.

Nutrition information

	Per recipe	***Per serving***
Kilocalories	2310 kcal	288.75 kcal
Protein	66.97 g	8.371 g
Carbohydrate	192.1 g	24.01 g
Fat	144.2 g	18.03 g
Cholesterol	563.9 mg	70.49 mg
Dietary fibre	1.03 g	0.13 g
Sodium	8.72 mg	1.09 mg
Iron	5708 mg	713.5mg

Fish coubouillon

(Dominica)

2 lb (908 g) fish
1 hot pepper, chopped
juice of 2 limes
2 blades of chive, chopped
1 garlic clove, crushed
4 tbsp oil
2 oz (56 g) margarine
1 tbsp flour

1. Clean the fish and marinate in a mixture of ½ pint (280 ml) water, salt, chopped hot pepper and the juice of 1 lime. Leave for 2 hours.
2. Lightly cook the chopped chives and crushed garlic in the oil and margarine.
3. Add the fish with the seasoned liquid and allow to cook for 10–15 minutes.
4. Blend the flour with 2 tablespoons water and add to the liquid.
5. Add the remaining lime juice, and season with salt and pepper to taste.

Serves: 6

Nutrition information

	Per recipe	*Per serving*
Kilocalories	2115.6 kcal	352.6 kcal
Protein	241.2 g	40.2 g
Carbohydrate	13.98 g	2.33 g
Fat	116.88 g	19.48 g
Cholesterol	426.9 mg	71.15 mg
Dietary fibre	0.66 g	0.11 g
Sodium	2121.6 mg	353.6 mg
Iron	2.76 mg	0.46 mg

Fish coubouillon (page 159)

Pigeon peas pinwheel

(Guyana)

1½ lb (681 g) cassava
1 tsp salt
2 tbsp margarine
2 oz (56 g) flour
4 oz (113 g) green pigeon peas
2 tbsp chopped seasonings
1 wiri-wiri pepper
4 tbsp tomato ketchup
1 egg, beaten

1. Prepare the cassava pastry. Wash and peel the cassava. Cut in halves and put to boil with the salt.
2. When cooked, remove the cassava and crush until lumps are removed. Add 1 tablespoon margarine and the flour and knead to a smooth pastry.
3. Prepare the filling. Wash the pigeon peas. Boil for 10 minutes. Drain.
4. Sauté the pigeon peas in 1 tablespoon margarine, add the chopped seasonings, wiri-wiri pepper, ketchup and salt to taste and cook for a few minutes.
5. Roll out the cassava pastry on a lightly floured board to ½ inch (1 cm) thick. Cut into rectangular shapes.
6. Put a portion of the pigeon pea mixture on each rectangle and fold into a roll. Baste with beaten egg.
7. Place in a hot oven, 400°F, for 20 minutes.
8. Remove from the oven, put to cool, then cut in 1-inch (2.5-cm) pinwheels.
9. Garnish as desired.

Makes: 12

Nutrition information

	Per recipe	*Per serving*
Kilocalories	1914 kcal	159.5 kcal
Protein	29.23 g	2.435 g
Carbohydrate	347.6 g	29 g
Fat	49.38 g	4.11 g
Cholesterol	0 mg	0 mg
Dietary fibre	3.716 g	0.309 g
Sodium	2326 mg	194 mg
Iron	10.24 mg	0.85 mg

Salt fish and vegetables in rice ball

(Guyana)

12 oz (340 g) cooked rice
2 tbsp chopped seasonings
1 wiri-wiri pepper, chopped
1 egg, beaten
4 tbsp milk
oil for deep frying
lettuce, tomatoes and onion rings to serve

For the filling:
2 oz (56 g) bora (string beans), cut in ½-inch (0.5-cm) pieces
2 oz (56 g) pumpkin, diced
1 small sweet pepper, chopped
2 oz (56 g) sweetcorn kernels
1 tbsp vegetable oil
4 oz (113 g) frizzled salt fish

For the coating:
3 eggs, beaten
4 oz (113 g) cheese, grated
4 oz (113 g) breadcrumbs

1. Place the rice in a basin and crush.
2. Add seasonings, pepper, egg, milk and black pepper to taste.
3. Sauté the vegetables for the filling in the oil and add the salt fish.
4. Season to taste, adding black pepper if necessary.
5. Divide rice mixture into five. Flatten each piece and add filling.
6. Roll and shape into neat balls.
7. Dip each ball in beaten egg and coat with cheese and breadcrumbs.
8. Deep fry until golden brown. Drain well.
9. Serve on a bed of lettuce with tomatoes and onion rings.

Makes: 5

To make rice more fluffy simply add 1 teaspoon lemon juice to every 2 pints (1.1 litres) of cooking water.

Nutrition information

	Per recipe	*Per serving*
Kilocalories	1897 kcal	379 kcal
Protein	60.94 g	12.19 g
Carbohydrate	175.4 g	35.1 g
Fat	106.7 g	21.3 g
Cholesterol	308.6 mg	61.7 mg
Dietary fibre	6.81 g	1.34 g
Sodium	1344 mg	265 mg
Iron	12.66 mg	2.53 mg

Shrimperi loaf

(Guyana)

12 oz (340 g) rice flour
4 oz (113 g) parboiled pigeon peas
5 oz (140 g) bora (string beans), cut into ¼-inch (0.5-cm) lengths
2 tbsp chopped eschallot
1 tsp chopped celery
¼ tsp chopped wiri-wiri pepper
4 oz (113 g) cooked shrimp
¼ pint (140 ml) cooking oil
2 eggs, beaten

1. Mix the rice flour with enough water to form a smooth thick paste.
2. Add the pigeon peas, bora, eschallot, celery and pepper.
3. Add the shrimp, oil and enough salt to taste. Fold in the beaten eggs.
4. Grease and line a loaf pan and pour in the mixture. Cover with foil or greaseproof paper.
5. Bake in a moderate oven, 350°F, for about 40–50 minutes.
6. Leave to cool and serve on a platter.

Serves: 8

To make celery crisp, let it stand in cold water to which 1 teaspoon sugar per 2 pints (1.1 litres) has been added.

Nutrition information

	Per recipe	***Per serving***
Kilocalories	2244 kcal	281 kcal
Protein	51.39 g	6.42 g
Carbohydrate	226.9 g	28.4 g
Fat	125.2 g	15.7 g
Cholesterol	551 mg	69 mg
Dietary fibre	6.703 g	0.838 g
Sodium	1359 mg	169.88 mg
Iron	6.65 mg	0.83 mg

Sweet salt fish cakes

(Guyana)

1½ lb (681 g) half-ripe plantains
1 lb (454 g) salt fish
1 oz (28 g) margarine
2 tbsp mustard
1 garlic clove, chopped
1 small onion, chopped
3 eggs
8 oz (227 g) breadcrumbs or biscuit crumbs
1 pint (560 ml) vegetable oil

1. Peel the plantains.
2. Boil the salt fish and plantains separately. Drain.
3. Mash the plantains with the margarine. Flake the salt fish.
4. Add the salt fish to the mashed plantain, then combine with the mustard, garlic, onion and 1 egg.
5. Mix well and form into cakes.
6. Heat the oil.
7. Beat the remaining eggs. Coat the fish cakes in beaten egg and crumbs and fry in the hot oil until brown.
8. Drain and serve.

Makes: 8

Nutrition information

	Per recipe	*Per serving*
Kilocalories	3804 kcal	476 kcal
Protein	208.1 g	26.01 g
Carbohydrate	375.6 g	46.9 g
Fat	167.1 g	20.9 g
Cholesterol	1013 mg	127 mg
Dietary fibre	16.74 g	2.09 g
Sodium	3271 mg	409 mg
Iron	23.05 mg	2.88 mg

Vegetarian roll

(Guyana)

¾ pint (420 ml) split peas
1 onion, finely chopped
1 tbsp finely chopped eschallot
7 young eddo leaves
oil for frying

1. Wash the peas and soak overnight.
2. Drain off the water and grind the peas, using an all-purpose mill.
3. Add the onion, eschallot, and salt and pepper to taste to the peas. Mix thoroughly.
4. Remove the stem and midrib from each eddo leaf. Wash, pat dry and lay flat on a pastry board.
5. Spread the mixture evenly between the leaves. Roll individually, and tie each leaf securely with string.
6. Place each roll into a plastic bag, then tie the opening.
7. Put the bags into a pot of boiling water and cook for 30–35 minutes.
8. Remove the rolls from the plastic bags and cut into 1½-inch (3.5-cm) thick slices.
9. Fry in hot oil until golden brown.

Serves: 7

Serve hot with vegetables or a savoury sauce.

Nutrition information

	Per recipe	*Per serving*
Kilocalories	1424 kcal	203 kcal
Protein	60.78 g	8.68 g
Carbohydrate	153.6 g	21.9 g
Fat	68.26 g	9.75 g
Cholesterol	134.3 mg	19.2 mg
Dietary fibre	29.61 g	4.23 g
Sodium	943.3 mg	134.8 mg
Iron	10.98 mg	1.57 mg

Zesty legume loaf

(Guyana)

8 oz (227 g) red peas
4 oz (113 g) black-eye peas
1 wiri-wiri pepper
1 blade of eschallot
1 onion
1 garlic clove
4 oz (113 g) breadcrumbs
4 oz (113 g) roasted peanuts, chopped
2 eggs

1. Wash the peas and soak overnight in a bowl of water. (The water must cover the peas by 2 inches/5 cm.)
2. Drain peas, then cook in a pot of boiling water until tender. Drain.
3. Wash the wiri-wiri pepper and eschallot. Peel the onion and garlic. Chop the garlic, onion, eschallot and pepper finely together.
4. Crush the cooked peas, add the chopped seasonings, salt to taste, the breadcrumbs and nuts.
5. Beat the eggs lightly and add to the peas mixture, binding well together.
6. Put the mixture into a greased loaf pan and bake in a moderate oven, 350°F, for 30 minutes or until brown.
7. Allow to cool, and serve on a platter with an appropriate garnish.

Serves: 6

When peeling onions, put the onions in cold water for half an hour before peeling and this will help prevent irritation to the eyes. Alternatively, peel the onions under a running cold tap.

Nutrition information

	Per recipe	***Per serving***
Kilocalories	2009 kcal	335 kcal
Protein	104.6 g	17.4 g
Carbohydrate	240.5 g	40.1 g
Fat	76.62 g	12.77 g
Cholesterol	426 mg	71 mg
Dietary fibre	46.39 g	7.73 g
Sodium	2575 mg	429 mg
Iron	25.42 mg	4.24 mg

Baked goods and sweet flavours

Breads, muffins and pancakes

Bran sweet potato loaf
Cheese cups
Cinnamon lentil loaf
Katy's breakfast muffins
Nutty butternut squash loaf
Nutty pumpkin bread
Pineapple muffins
Pineapple rolls
Potato bread
Pumpkin pancakes
Spinach nut loaf
Tutti frutti loaf

Other baked goods

Black-eye buns
Black-eye cookies
Breadfruit caramel cake
Breadfruit pastry
Breadfruit pizza (vegetarian)
Breadfruit pone
Golden apple 'n' cream sponge cake
Hummingbird cake
Nature's layered guava cake
Guava icing
Pineapple coconut bars
Ripe breadfruit cake

Sweet flavours

Hibiscusade
Peppermint liqueur
Peppermints

Breads, muffins and pancakes

'Ye shall bring out of your habitations two wave loaves of two tenth deals: they shall be of fine flour; they shall be baken with leaven; they are the first fruits unto the Lord' – *Leviticus 23: 17*

Bread is the breakfast staple in the Caribbean and is of a heavier texture than is known elsewhere. This includes the famous hard dough bread of the Jamaicans. It is believed that this type of bread was devised by the slaves, who tried to make it of a more solid texture in order to satisfy themselves in the same manner as with the provisions which they had originally eaten in the mornings.

Generally breadstuff in the Caribbean includes white bread, hard dough, butter bread, Johnny cakes, bakes, roti and pancakes. This section features breads which have been developed using indigenous ingredients.

Bran sweet potato loaf

(Barbados)

12 oz (340 g) wholewheat flour
4 oz (113 g) bran flakes
3 tsp baking powder
2 tsp cinnamon
1 tsp salt
4 oz (113 g) margarine
4 oz (113 g) dark sugar
6 oz (168 g) sweet potato, cooked and mashed
1 egg, beaten
½ pint (280 ml) milk

1. Mix the dry ingredients in a bowl.
2. Rub the fat into the flour until the mixture looks like fine breadcrumbs.
3. Add the sugar and the mashed sweet potato.
4. Make a well in the centre of the mixture and add the beaten egg.
5. Mix to a stiff dough, adding milk as necessary.
6. Put into a greased loaf pan and bake in a hot oven, 400°F, for about 35–40 minutes until the loaf is done.

Serves: 6

Nutrition information

	Per recipe	*Per serving*
Kilocalories	2850 kcal	475 kcal
Protein	76.64 g	12.77g
Carbohydrate	402.2 g	67 g
Fat	113.7 g	18.95 g
Cholesterol	246 mg	41 mg
Dietary fibre	20.28 g	3.38 g
Sodium	5297 mg	882.63 mg
Iron	48.49 mg	8.08 mg

Cheese cups

(Guyana)

8 oz (227 g) plain rice flour
4 tsp baking powder
2 oz (56 g) margarine
4 oz (113 g) cottage cheese or grated cheese
¼ tsp pepper sauce
1 tsp mustard
¼ tsp salt
2 eggs, beaten
¼ pint (140 ml) milk

1. Sieve the flour and baking powder.
2. Cream the margarine and cheese.
3. Add the pepper sauce, mustard, salt and eggs to the margarine mixture.
4. Fold in the flour and enough milk to form a dropping consistency.
5. Pour the mixture into greased muffin pans and bake in a hot oven, 400°F, for 15 minutes or until cooked.

Makes: 12

Nutrition information

	Per recipe	*Per serving*
Kilocalories	2080 kcal	173 kcal
Protein	71.29 g	5.94 g
Carbohydrate	280 g	23.3 g
Fat	73.02 g	6.09 g
Cholesterol	478 mg	39.83 mg
Dietary fibre	6.163 g	0.51 g
Sodium	3741 mg	311.75 mg
Iron	4.993 mg	0.416 mg

Cinnamon lentil loaf

(Barbados)

8 oz (227 g) wholewheat flour
2 tsp baking powder
2 tsp cinnamon
½ tsp mixed spice
⅛ tsp salt
4 oz (113 g) margarine
4 oz (113 g) sugar
6 oz (168 g) lentils, boiled and crushed
1 egg
¼ tsp vanilla essence
½ pint (280 ml) milk
glacé cherries, to decorate

1. Sieve together the flour, baking powder, cinnamon, spice and salt.
2. Rub the margarine into the dry ingredients until the mixture resembles fine breadcrumbs.
3. Add the sugar and crushed lentils to the mixture.
4. Beat the egg with the vanilla essence.
5. Make a well in the centre of the mixture and add the beaten egg and milk, a little at a time, while mixing.
6. Knead well, place in a greased loaf pan and decorate with cherries
7. Bake for 40–45 minutes at 375°F. Test with a skewer for readiness.
8. Cool on a wire rack

Serves: 6

Nutrition information

	Per recipe	***Per serving***
Kilocalories	2302 kcal	384 kcal
Protein	63.34 g	10.56 g
Carbohydrate	270.9 g	45.15 g
Fat	111.3 g	18.55 g
Cholesterol	246 mg	41 mg
Dietary fibre	9.217 g	1.54 g
Sodium	2293 mg	382.16 mg
Iron	20.49 mg	3.42 mg

Wilton

Katy's breakfast muffins

(Trinidad)

3 eggs
10 fl oz (350 ml) milk
5 tbsp melted margarine
1½ oz (42 g) bran flakes
1 lb (454 g) plain flour, sifted
2 oz (56 g) sugar
4 oz (113 g) Cheddar cheese, grated
½ onion, chopped
8 oz (227 g) pimentos, chopped
4 tbsp chopped ham, salami or sausage meat
3 oz (84 g) carrots, grated

1. Beat the eggs lightly.
2. Combine the milk, eggs, melted margarine and bran in a bowl. Set aside for 30 minutes.
3. Add all the other ingredients and mix enough to moisten.
4. Spoon into greased muffin pans.
5. Bake at 450°F for 15–20 minutes.

Makes: 16

These freeze well and serve as a complete breakfast item.

Nutrition information

	Per recipe	*Per serving*
Kilocalories	2633.6 kcal	164.6 kcal
Protein	95.01 g	5.938 g
Carbohydrate	277.92 g	17.37 g
Fat	127.68 g	7.98 g
Cholesterol	818.56 mg	51.16 mg
Dietary fibre	12.64 g	0.79 g
Sodium	2480 mg	155 mg
Iron	17.79 mg	1.112 mg

Nutty butternut squash loaf

(Barbados)

8 oz (227 g) squash
8 oz (227 g) flour
1½ tsp baking powder
1 tbsp mixed spice
¼ tsp salt
2 oz (56 g) margarine
3 oz (84 g) sugar
1 oz (28 g) ground almonds
1 oz (28 g) raisins
2 eggs, beaten
½ tsp vanilla essence

1. Boil the squash, drain and crush.
2. Sieve together the flour, baking powder, spice and salt.
3. Rub in the margarine until the mixture resembles fine breadcrumbs.
4. Stir in the sugar with a fork, then add the almonds, raisins and squash and mix well.
5. Whisk eggs and essence together and add enough to the mixture to form a soft dough.
6. Place in a greased loaf pan, sprinkle with sugar and bake at 350°F for 30–40 minutes or until cooked.

Serves: 6

Pumpkin may replace the squash and peanuts may be used instead of almonds.

Nutrition information

	Per recipe	***Per serving***
Kilocalories	2014 kcal	335.66 kcal
Protein	52.69 g	8.78 g
Carbohydrate	290.14 g	48.36 g
Fat	75.77 g	12.62 g
Cholesterol	613.76 mg	102.29 mg
Dietary fibre	13.39 g	2.23 g
Sodium	1815 mg	302.5 mg
Iron	17.72 mg	2.95 mg

Nutty pumpkin bread

(Antigua)

1 tsp active dry yeast
12 fl oz (210 ml) lukewarm water
1 lb (454 g) pumpkin, cooked and mashed
2 tbsp sugar
1 egg, beaten
1 lb (454 g) plain flour
1 tsp salt
2 oz vegetable oil
2 oz (56 g) pumpkin seeds
1 tbsp melted margarine

1. Dissolve the yeast in 5 tablespoons lukewarm water.
2. Add the remaining water, the mashed pumpkin, sugar, beaten egg and half the flour to the yeast mixture and beat well.
3. Place in a lightly greased bowl, cover and leave in a warm place to rise until double in size, about 30 minutes. Punch down.
4. Add the salt to the remaining flour and mix well.
5. Add the oil to the dough and mix well, then add the flour and pumpkin seeds. Continue mixing.
6. Turn out on a lightly floured board and knead.
7. Replace in the bowl and leave to rise for 25 minutes.
8. Punch down and place in a 12-inch (30-cm) loaf pan. Allow to rise until double in bulk.
9. Bake at 350°F for 1 hour.
10. Glaze the top with melted margarine.

Serves: 8

Strong plain flour is the best for yeast recipes as it absorbs liquid easily and kneads quickly into a firm dough.

Nutrition information

	Per recipe	***Per serving***
Kilocalories	2845 kcal	356 kcal
Protein	61.67 g	7.71 g
Carbohydrate	395.7 g	49.46 g
Fat	111 g	13.87 g
Cholesterol	337.1 mg	42.13 mg
Dietary fibre	22 g	2.74 g
Sodium	2682 mg	335.25 mg
Iron	22.6 mg	2.82 mg

Pineapple muffins

(Antigua)

8 oz (227 g) flour
1 oz (28 g) sugar
1 tbsp baking powder
½ tsp salt
2 eggs, beaten
½ pint (280 ml) pineapple juice
2 oz (56 g) melted butter or margarine
3 oz (84 g) pineapple chunks, well drained

1. Mix the flour, sugar, baking powder and salt together.
2. In a small bowl, combine the beaten eggs, juice and melted butter.
3. Add the liquid ingredients all at once to the dry ingredients. Add the pineapple chunks.
4. Stir quickly until the ingredients are just mixed and the batter is lumpy in appearance.
5. Fill greased muffin pans two-thirds full with the batter.
6. Bake at 400°F for 20–25 minutes.
7. Serve warm.

Makes: 12

Nutrition information

	Per recipe	*Per serving*
Kilocalories	1756.8 kcal	146.4 kcal
Protein	39.99 g	3.333 g
Carbohydrate	266.64 g	22.22 g
Fat	58.8 g	4.9 g
Cholesterol	426 mg	35.5 mg
Dietary fibre	8.64 g	0.72 g
Sodium	2826 mg	235.5 mg
Iron	14.16 mg	1.18 mg

Pineapple rolls

(Antigua)

2 tbsp active dry yeast
4 oz (113 g) sugar plus 2 tsp
¼ pint (140 ml) warm water
½ pint (280 ml) milk
2 tsp salt
2 oz (56 g) margarine
2 eggs
2 lb (908 g) plain flour
10 oz (280 g) pineapple chunks (see below)

1. Set the yeast using 2 teaspoons sugar and ¼ pint (140 ml) warm water.
2. Scald milk, stir in remaining sugar and salt, then add 6 fl oz (210 ml) cold water.
3. Add the milk mixture, the margarine, eggs and 8 oz (227 g) flour to the dissolved yeast mixture. Beat until smooth.
4. Drain the pineapple chunks thoroughly and mix with 4 oz (113 g) flour. Coat well and add to the dough. Add the remaining flour gradually.
5. Mix to form a soft dough which leaves the sides of the bowl.
6. Turn onto a floured board and knead for 5–10 minutes or until the dough becomes smooth and elastic and is no longer sticky.
7. Place in a lightly greased bowl. Grease the top of the dough. Cover and put to rise in a warm place until double in size, about 1 hour.
8. Punch down, turn out onto a board, and cut into four equal portions. Divide each portion into six. Shape into rolls and place on a greased baking sheet. Put to rise in a warm place until double in size.
9. Bake at 370° F for about 12–15 minutes.
10. Brush with a sugar glaze 5 minutes before the end of baking time.

Makes: 24

If fresh pineapple is used, it should be scalded first to inactivate the enzyme bromelin which breaks down protein.

Nutrition information

	Per recipe	***Per serving***
Kilocalories	5311 kcal	221.3 kcal
Protein	162.72 g	6.78 g
Carbohydrate	964.8 g	40.2 g
Fat	84.72 g	3.53 g
Cholesterol	459.12 mg	19.13 mg
Dietary fibre	44.64 g	1.86 g
Sodium	5080 mg	211.7 mg
Iron	55.2 mg	2.3 mg

Pineapples (see page 177)

Potato bread

(St Vincent and the Grenadines)

2 tbsp active dry yeast
½ pint (280 ml) warm water
1 tbsp sugar
2 tbsp vegetable oil
1 tsp salt
1 lb (454 g) seasoned mashed potato
1 lb (454 g) plain flour
2 oz (56 g) margarine

1. Dissolve the yeast in the warm water with the sugar.
2. Add the oil, salt and mashed potato and mix thoroughly.
3. Add half the flour and beat well. Add enough flour to make a firm dough and knead until smooth.
4. Cover the dough and allow to rise until double in size. Place in loaf pans and let rise again.
5. Bake for about 1 hour in a moderate oven, 350°F.

Serves: 6

Always cover dough well during rising to prevent a skin forming on the surface.

Nutrition information

	Per recipe	***Per serving***
Kilocalories	2910 kcal	485 kcal
Protein	69.38 g	11.56 g
Carbohydrate	477.3 g	79.55 g
Fat	81 g	13.5 g
Cholesterol	8 mg	1.33 mg
Dietary fibre	21.92 g	3.65 g
Sodium	4037 mg	672.83 mg
Iron	24.97 mg	4.16 mg

Pumpkin pancakes

(Guyana)

4 oz (113 g) plain rice flour
2 tsp baking powder
½ tsp salt
1 tsp sugar
8 oz (227 g) pumpkin, boiled and mashed
½ pint (280 ml) milk and water, mixed
2 tbsp oil

1. Mix all the dry ingredients.
2. Add the mashed pumpkin and blend well.
3. Add the combined milk and water to the mixture.
4. Beat well until bubbles appear on the surface.
5. Using a ladle, pour the mixture onto a greased hot griddle. Cook until bubbles appear.
6. Turn the pancake over and brown the other side.

Makes: 1 large pancake or 8 individual pancakes

Use about 4 tablespoons of batter to make individual pancakes.

Nutrition information

	Per recipe	*Per serving*
Kilocalories	940.3 kcal	117.5 kcal
Protein	14.31 g	1.79 g
Carbohydrate	145.4 g	18.17 g
Fat	33.65 g	4.21 g
Cholesterol	16.5 mg	2.06 mg
Dietary fibre	6.34 g	0.79 g
Sodium	3991 mg	499 mg
Iron	2.438 mg	0.30 mg

Spinach nut loaf

(Barbados)

8 oz (227 g) wholewheat flour
2 tsp baking powder
1 tsp mixed spice
4 oz (113 g) margarine
3 oz (84 g) sugar
3 oz (84 g) nuts, chopped
1 egg, beaten
¼ tsp vanilla essence
4 tbsp milk
6 oz (168 g) spinach, finely chopped

1. Sieve together the flour, baking powder and spice.
2. Rub the margarine into the flour until the mixture resembles fine breadcrumbs.
3. Add the sugar and chopped nuts. Stir with a fork.
4. Add the egg together with the vanilla essence and milk.
5. Add the spinach and mix well.
6. Place into a greased 12-inch (30-cm) loaf pan.
7. Bake at 375°F for 40 minutes or until cooked. Test with a skewer for readiness.
8. Cool on a wire rack.

Serves: 6

Nutrition information

	Per recipe	*Per serving*
Kilocalories	2390 kcal	398 kcal
Protein	61.2 g	10.2 g
Carbohydrate	220 g	36.66 g
Fat	148.62 g	24.78 g
Cholesterol	221.2 mg	36.86 mg
Dietary fibre	10.96 g	1.83 g
Sodium	2050 mg	341.6 mg
Iron	21.54 mg	3.6 mg

Tutti frutti loaf

(Guyana)

8 oz (227 g) plain rice flour
3 tsp baking powder
3 oz (84 g) margarine
4 oz (113 g) sugar
1 tsp cinnamon
4 tbsp coarsely chopped pineapple
4 tbsp chopped dried fruit
4 tbsp chopped red and green preserved papaw
4 tbsp chopped peanuts
4 eggs, beaten
milk

1. Sieve the flour and baking powder into a bowl.
2. Rub the margarine into the flour until the mixture resembles fine breadcrumbs.
3. Add the sugar, cinnamon, fruit and nuts.
4. Mix with the beaten eggs and enough milk to form a soft dough.
5. Place into a greased loaf pan.
6. Bake at 350°F for 35–40 minutes.

Serves: 10

Nutrition information

	Per recipe	*Per serving*
Kilocalories	2926 kcal	293 kcal
Protein	55.87 g	5.59 g
Carbohydrate	440.3 g	44.03 g
Fat	113.1 g	11.31 g
Cholesterol	852 mg	85.2 mg
Dietary fibre	27.93 g	2.79 g
Sodium	2521 mg	252.1 mg
Iron	10.35 mg	1.04 mg

Other baked goods

Black-eye buns

(Guyana)

4 oz (113 g) margarine
4 oz (113 g) sugar
1 tsp mixed spice or cinnamon
a pinch of salt
2 tbsp honey
2 tbsp molasses
8 oz (227 g) black-eye peas, cooked and mashed
2 oz (56 g) mixed dried fruit
8 oz (227 g) flour
2 tsp baking powder

1. Melt the margarine and mix with the sugar.
2. Add the spice, salt, honey and molasses and mix well.
3. Add the mashed peas and fruits and mix thoroughly.
4. Sift together the flour and baking powder. Fold into the mixture and mix well to remove lumps.
5. Place even-sized portions into greased muffin pans and bake at 350°F for 35 minutes.
6. When the muffins are done, turn onto a wire rack and glaze with honey.

Makes: 9

Nutrition information

	Per recipe	*Per serving*
Kilocalories	3753 kcal	417.8 kcal
Protein	132.12 g	14.68 g
Carbohydrate	592.65 g	65.85 g
Fat	104.13 g	11.57 g
Cholesterol	0 mg	0 mg
Dietary fibre	134.37 g	14.93 g
Sodium	2561.4 mg	284.6 mg
Iron	37.836 mg	4.204 mg

Black-eye cookies

(Guyana)

4 oz (113 g) flour
1 tsp baking powder
6 oz (168 g) black-eye peas, cooked and mashed
4 oz (113 g) brown sugar
4 oz (113 g) margarine
¼ tsp vanilla essence

1. Sift together the flour and baking powder into a mixing bowl.
2. Add the other ingredients and mix thoroughly until the mixture holds together.
3. Place on a lightly floured board and roll out to ⅛-inch (0.25-cm) thickness.
4. Cut into shapes with a 1½-inch (3.5-cm) cookie cutter.
5. Place on a lightly greased baking sheet and bake at 350°F for 20 minutes or until lightly brown.

Makes: 40

Nutrition information

	Per recipe	*Per serving*
Kilocalories	1845 kcal	46.125 kcal
Protein	26.433 g	0.661 g
Carbohydrate	229.59 g	5.74 g
Fat	93.69 g	2.342 g
Cholesterol	0 mg	0 mg
Dietary fibre	19.58 g	0.489 g
Sodium	1606.5 mg	40.163 mg
Iron	9.09 mg	0.227 mg

Black-eye cookies (page 185)

Breadfruit caramel cake

(Barbados)

1¼ lb (567 g) breadfruit, just under-ripe
4 oz (113 g) coconut
4 eggs
1 tsp cinnamon
4 oz (113 g) sugar
¼ pint (140 ml) caramel
5 oz (140 g) dried fruit, chopped
4 tsp mixed essence
¼–½ pint (140–280 ml) water
4 tsp baking powder
4 tbsp wine or rum (optional)

1. Grate the breadfruit and coconut.
2. Mix all the ingredients except the baking powder, water and wine.
3. Beat vigorously until the sugar dissolves.
4. Add enough water to make a pouring consistency.
5. Add the baking powder and stir.
6. Pour the mixture into a greased cake pan.
7. Bake at 300°F for about 1 hour or until set.
8. Sprinkle with wine or rum if desired.
9. Allow to cool before removing from the pan.

Serves: 12

Nutrition information

	Per recipe	***Per serving***
Kilocalories	2106 kcal	175.6 kcal
Protein	35.16 g	2.93 g
Carbohydrate	358.1 g	29.84 g
Fat	49.66 g	4.14 g
Cholesterol	852 mg	71 mg
Dietary fibre	11.09 g	0.92 g
Sodium	1856 mg	154.67 mg
Iron	32.94 mg	2.74 mg

Breadfruit pastry

(Barbados)

1 small breadfruit
about ¼ tsp salt
1 oz (28 g) flour

1. Boil the breadfruit and crush until fine and smooth. Add salt to taste.
2. Sprinkle a pastry board with the flour and knead the breadfruit until smooth.
3. Continue to knead until the dough no longer sticks.
4. Roll out the dough and use as pastry casing/shell.

Makes: 1 x 8-inch (20-cm) pie shell
Serves: 8

For biscuits, add fruit or other flavourings to the mixture, cut into shapes and bake.

Nutrition information

	Per recipe	*Per serving*
Kilocalories	978.4 kcal	134.8 kcal
Protein	27.776 g	3.472 g
Carbohydrate	228.48 g	28.56g
Fat	3.552 g	0.444 g
Cholesterol	0 mg	0 mg
Dietary fibre	7.24 g	0.905 g
Sodium	4656.8 mg	582.1 mg
Iron	15.024 mg	1.878 mg

Breadfruit pizza (vegetarian)

(Guyana)

1 small ripe breadfruit (not soft)
1 small bundle of eschallots
2 garlic cloves
2 onions
2 tsp baking power
2 eggs
4 oz (113 g) flour
1 tbsp margarine, softened
1 tbsp mustard
1 tbsp tomato ketchup
8 oz (227 g) cheese, grated
8 oz (227 g) carrots, shredded
½ pint (280 ml) boiled black-eye peas
1 can sweetcorn
4 sweet peppers (2 green, 1 yellow, 1 red), sliced
1 firm red tomato, sliced

1. Boil the breadfruit and crush until smooth while still hot.
2. Chop the eschallots, garlic and 1 onion finely. Add to the breadfruit with the baking powder and salt to taste. Mix well.
3. Beat the eggs lightly, add to the mixture, and mix to a stiff dough.
4. Sprinkle a board with the flour and knead the mixture gently. Set aside.
5. Grease a pizza pan. Roll the dough out thinly and line the pan.
6. Brush the dough with the margarine, mustard and tomato ketchup.
7. Sprinkle with half the cheese.
8. Slice the remaining onion and arrange attractively with the carrots, black-eye peas and sweetcorn on top of the cheese.
9. Top with the remaining cheese, the sweet peppers and tomato.
10. Bake at 475°F for 20 minutes or until the dough is lightly brown.

Serves: 8

Nutrition information

	Per recipe	*Per serving*
Kilocalories	3016.8 kcal	377.1 kcal
Protein	93.52 g	11.69 g
Carbohydrate	437.52 g	54.69 g
Fat	97.12 g	12.14g
Cholesterol	665.6 mg	83.2 mg
Dietary fibre	35.2 g	4.4 g
Sodium	7711 mg	963.9 mg
Iron	38.08 mg	4.76 mg

Breadfruit pone

(Barbados)

1¼ lb (567 g) breadfruit, grated
4 oz (113 g) grated coconut
1 tsp salt
5 oz (140 g) sugar
3 tbsp margarine
2 oz (56 g) flour
¼ tsp nutmeg
½ tsp cinnamon
½ tsp vanilla essence
¼ pint (140 ml) milk

1. Mix all the ingredients thoroughly.
2. Pour into a greased baking dish or pan and bake in a moderate oven, 350°F, for 40–50 minutes. When done, a knife inserted should come out clean.
3. Serve either hot or cold as a dessert or snack.

Serves: 12

Nutrition information

	Per recipe	*Per serving*
Kilocalories	1841 kcal	153.4 kcal
Protein	18.92 g	1.58 g
Carbohydrate	299.4 g	24.95 g
Fat	66.78 g	5.57 g
Cholesterol	16.5 mg	1.37 mg
Dietary fibre	9.01 g	0.75 g
Sodium	2690 mg	224 mg
Iron	24.66 mg	2.05 mg

Golden apple 'n' cream sponge cake

(St Kitts)

4 oz (113 g) plain flour, sifted
1 tsp baking powder
½ tsp salt
¼ pint (140 ml) milk
2 tsp margarine
3 eggs
8 oz (227 g) white sugar
1 tsp vanilla essence
½ pint (280 ml) heavy cream
½ pint (280 ml) stewed golden apple
cherries, to decorate

1. Sift together the flour, baking powder and salt.
2. Heat the milk and margarine until small bubbles appear around the edge (do not boil). Allow to cool.
3. Beat the eggs in a small bowl until foamy. Gradually beat in the sugar until the mixture is very thick and fluffy.
4. Beat in the vanilla essence and cooled milk.
5. Fold the flour mixture gently into the egg mixture until well blended.
6. Pour batter into two greased and floured 9-inch (22.5-cm) sandwich pans.
7. Bake in a moderate oven, 350°F, for 25 minutes until done.
8. Cool in pans for 10 minutes, then remove and cool completely on a wire rack.
9. Beat the cream in a small bowl until firm peaks are formed.
10. Place one cake layer on a serving plate. Spread with half the whipped cream and top with the golden apple.
11. Top with the remaining cake layer. Decorate with the remaining whipped cream and some cherries.

Serves: 10

Use mangoes, pineapple or guavas in place of golden apple.

Nutrition information

	Per recipe	*Per serving*
Kilocalories	2863 kcal	286 kcal
Protein	41.44 g	4.14 g
Carbohydrate	420.6 g	42.06 g
Fat	116.8 g	11.68 g
Cholesterol	981.5 mg	98.15 mg
Dietary fibre	8.335 g	0.83 g
Sodium	1863 mg	186.3 mg
Iron	15.64 mg	1.56 mg

Hummingbird cake

(Barbados)

8 oz (227 g) flour
½ tsp cinnamon
½ tsp salt
½ tsp baking soda
8 oz (227 g) sugar
12 fl oz (210 ml) vegetable oil
1 tsp vanilla essence
2 eggs, beaten
3 oz (84 g) crushed pineapple
1 lb (454 g) bananas, mashed
1 oz (28 g) chopped nuts

1. Sieve the flour, cinnamon, salt and baking soda together into a bowl.
2. Add the sugar, vegetable oil, vanilla essence, beaten eggs and pineapple. Mix well with a wooden spoon.
3. Fold in the banana and nuts.
4. Turn into a greased and floured deep 10-inch (25-cm) diameter cake pan and bake in a moderate oven, 350°F, for about 1 hour.
5. Leave in the pan for about 15 minutes before turning out on a wire rack to cool completely.

Serves: 12

Nutrition information

	Per recipe	***Per serving***
Kilocalories	4297 kcal	358 kcal
Protein	58.74 g	4.89 g
Carbohydrate	533.3 g	44.4 g
Fat	226 g	19 g
Cholesterol	426 mg	35.5 mg
Dietary fibre	22.84 g	1.9 g
Sodium	1926 mg	160.5 mg
Iron	20.8 mg	1.73 mg

Guavas

Nature's layered guava cake

(Dominica)

8 oz (227 g) margarine
8 oz (227 g) sugar
1 lb (454 g) flour
4 tsp baking powder
3 eggs
½ tsp grated lime or lemon rind
½ pint (280 ml) milk
½ pint (280 ml) guava juice
½ pint (280 ml) stewed guavas
a little warmed guava jelly or jam
cherries or guava slices, to decorate

1. Cream the margarine and sugar together.
2. Sieve the flour and baking powder into a bowl.
3. Beat the eggs with the grated rind.
4. Add the eggs to the creamed mixture. Mix thoroughly.
5. Fold the flour gradually into the mixture, adding the milk and guava juice alternately.
6. Fold the stewed guavas into the mixture.
7. Divide the mixture between three greased and floured 9-inch (22.5-cm) sandwich pans.
8. Bake at 350°F for 30–35 minutes or until golden brown.
9. When the cakes are cooled, remove from the pans.
10. Spread a layer of guava jelly on the top of two cakes, and sandwich all three together.
11. Decorate with guava icing and cherries or guava slices.

Serves: 12

A cake is completely cooked when it springs back from a light touch or when a skewer inserted into the centre comes out clean.

Nutrition information

	Per recipe	*Per serving*
Kilocalories	4991 kcal	416 kcal
Protein	68.21 g	5.68 g
Carbohydrate	707.1 g	58.92 g
Fat	214.5g	17.88 g
Cholesterol	685.1 mg	57.09 mg
Dietary fibre	10.85 g	0.9 g
Sodium	4032 mg	336 mg
Iron	38.34 mg	3.2 mg

Guava icing

(Dominica)

3 oz (85 g) shortening
1 lb (454 g) icing sugar, sifted
2–4 tbsp guava juice
food colouring (optional)

1. Cream the shortening until soft.
2. Add the icing sugar gradually and soften with drops of guava juice until the correct consistency is reached. Colour as desired.
3. Spread over cake.

Serves: 12

Nutrition information

	Per recipe	***Per serving***
Kilocalories	2422 kcal	202 kcal
Protein	0 g	0 g
Carbohydrate	457.2 g	38.1 g
Fat	75 g	6.25 g
Cholesterol	0 mg	0 mg
Dietary fibre	0 g	0 g
Sodium	6.235 mg	0.52 mg
Iron	0.45 mg	0.04 mg

Pineapple coconut bars

(Antigua)

4 oz (113 g) butter or margarine
8 oz (227 g) firmly packed brown sugar
2 eggs
¼ tsp almond essence
3 oz (84 g) plain flour
¾ tsp baking powder
⅛ tsp salt
3 oz (84 g) grated coconut
8 oz (227 g) pineapple, finely chopped and well drained

1. Mix the butter and sugar in a large bowl until creamy.
2. Beat in the eggs and almond essence.
3. In another bowl, stir together the flour, baking powder and salt.
4. Gradually add the flour mixture to the butter mixture, blending thoroughly.
5. Stir in the grated coconut and chopped pineapple.
6. Spread the mixture evenly in a greased and floured 9-inch (22.5-cm) square baking pan.
7. Bake in a moderate oven, 350°F, for 25–30 minutes, or until the top springs back when lightly touched.
8. Leave to cool in the pan.
9. When cool, cut into bars, 1 x 2¼ inches (2.5 x 5.5 cm). Store in an airtight tin.

Makes: 36

These make a sweet treat with a delightful blend of flavours.

Nutrition information

	Per recipe	***Per serving***
Kilocalories	2464.8 kcal	68.47 kcal
Protein	26.05 g	0.72 g
Carbohydrate	325.32g	9.04 g
Fat	123.84 g	3.44 g
Cholesterol	426 mg	11.83 mg
Dietary fibre	10.84 g	0.3 g
Sodium	2787.6 mg	77.43 mg
Iron	11.89 mg	0.33 mg

Ripe breadfruit cake

(St Vincent and the Grenadines)

5 oz (140 g) flour
2 tsp baking powder
¼ tsp nutmeg
¼ tsp salt
4 oz (113 g) margarine
2 oz (56 g) brown sugar
2 eggs, beaten
1 tsp vanilla essence
½ pint (280 ml) mashed ripe breadfruit
1 tsp finely grated orange rind
2 tbsp orange juice

1. Sift the flour, baking powder, nutmeg and salt together.
2. Cream the margarine and sugar together until fluffy.
3. Add the beaten eggs one at a time, followed by the vanilla essence.
4. Beat in the mashed breadfruit and the orange rind.
5. Fold in the flour mixture in quarters, adding alternately with the orange juice to give a soft dropping consistency.
6. Put the mixture in a greased 6-inch (15-cm) diameter baking pan and bake at 375°F for about 45 minutes, or until golden brown and well done.
7. Leave in the pan for about 5 minutes, then turn out and cool on a rack.

Serves: 6

Nutrition information

	Per recipe	***Per serving***
Kilocalories	1949 kcal	324.8 kcal
Protein	21.8 g	3.63 g
Carbohydrate	219.3 g	36.55 g
Fat	104.3 g	17.38 g
Cholesterol	426 mg	71 mg
Dietary fibre	7.041 g	1.173 g
Sodium	2953 mg	492.17 mg
Iron	13.89 mg	2.32 mg

Sweet flavours

Hibiscusade

(St Croix)

30 single red hibiscus blooms
½ oz (14 g) ginger, grated or minced
juice of 6 limes
sugar

1. Wash the hibiscus and ginger.
2. Boil the ginger in 2 pints (1.1 litres) water for about 2 minutes.
3. Add the hibiscus, remove from heat and cover.
4. When cool, strain into a large pot.
5. Add 4 pints (3.3 litres) water and the lime juice. Sweeten to taste.
6. Chill and serve cold. If too thick, add more water and sugar to taste.

Serves: 12

If you wish, add a dash of rum or any liquor of your choice.

Nutrition information

	Per recipe	*Per serving*
Kilocalories	815.9 kcal	67.9 kcal
Protein	1.027 g	0.086 g
Carbohydrate	211.3 g	17.6 g
Fat	0.465 g	0.038 g
Cholesterol	0 mg	0 mg
Dietary fibre	0.399 g	0.033 g
Sodium	5.461mg	0.455 mg
Iron	0.869 mg	0.072 mg

Peppermint liqueur

(Barbados)

1 lb (454 g) sugar
1½ pints (840 ml) white rum
about 1 tsp peppermint oil

1. Put the sugar and rum into a clear jar.
2. Add the peppermint oil by the drop to suit your taste.
3. Allow to infuse for about 14 days until the sugar has dissolved.
4. Strain and bottle. The flavour improves with keeping.

Serves: 15

Peppermint oil is very strong, so add carefully.

Nutrition information

	Per recipe	*Per serving*
Kilocalories	3313 kcal	220.87 kcal
Protein	0 g	0 g
Carbohydrate	453.6 g	30.24 g
Fat	0.165 g	0.011 g
Cholesterol	0 mg	0 mg
Dietary fibre	0 g	0 g
Sodium	6.823 mg	0.455 mg
Iron	0.992 mg	0.066 mg

Peppermints

(Barbados)

1 egg white
thinly peeled rind of ½ orange or lime
1 lb (454 g) icing sugar, sifted
about ½ tsp peppermint oil
food colouring

1. Lightly heat the egg white with the rind, then remove the rind.
2. Add the sifted sugar little by little, mixing with a wooden spoon or spatula until the mixture is stiff enough to handle.
3. Add a few drops of peppermint oil to taste and mix well.
4. Divide the mixture into two or more portions, using a drop of food colouring of your choice.
5. Using your hands, roll out each portion on a pastry board well dusted with icing sugar.
6. Cut to size, using a sharp knife or kitchen scissors.
7. Place on a flat sheet to dry for about 12 hours.

Makes: 24

Nutrition information

	Per recipe	*Per serving*
Kilocalories	1840 kcal	76.67 kcal
Protein	6.25 g	0.26 g
Carbohydrate	454.2 g	18.93 g
Fat	5.093 g	0.212 g
Cholesterol	213 mg	8.875 mg
Dietary fibre	0 g	0 g
Sodium	69.81 mg	2.91 mg
Iron	0.992 mg	0.041 mg

Recipe composition tables

Traditional dishes

Recipe	Energy kcal	Protein g	Total fat g	Saturated fat g	Cholesterol mg	Carbohydrate (total) g	Dietary fibre g
ANGUILLA							
Baked eel	2657.6	168.52	214.16	35.84	1142	5.92	0.464
ANTIGUA AND BARBUDA							
Antigua Sunday morning breakfast	2160	307.4	73.9	13.58	1114	57.4	19.31
Antigua pepperpot	3833	306	179.3	45.51	491.4	275.2	46.22
Cornmeal – Fungee	1019	23.97	4.612	0.63	0	216.2	15.12
BAHAMAS							
Conch chowder	574.38	34.77	15.43	4.58	115.98	81.36	13.64
Chicken souse	3156	339.1	168.7	47.01	1315	50.12	4.754
Johnny cake	1879.8	26.77	94.44	57.9	248.52	231.18	7.2
Guava duff	2717.4	40.92	151.8	31.82	228.42	303.6	34.48
Hard sauce	3232	5.45	183.8	114.9	496.6	404.9	0
BARBADOS							
Flying fish melts in cheese sauce	1638	116.3	100.7	26.64	95.39	62.66	2.97
'Doved' peas	1968	115	53.76	14.53	65.65	264.3	1.57
Cou cou	1097	24.61	12.33	5.44	20.71	218.4	15.87
Jug-jug	20524	984.6	898.7	15.99	0	2186	519.6
Conkies	2838	55.31	61.16	37.94	442.5	532	38.86
BELIZE							
Arroz con pollo	3036.64	137.77	141.63	37.812	467.4	299.56	16.77
Letu banana mulsa	868.95	11.69	5.15	3.1	0	215.84	11.91
CAYMAN ISLANDS							
Zuppa di pesce	520	77.24	14.09	3.16	288.1	17.04	1.19
Beer-batter fish	2222.4	186.24	94	5.42	0	122.24	5.04
Coconut cream pie	3425	51.84	216.2	115.6	1034	311.7	12.79
Banana mudslide	428.8	3.50	5.18	2.82	34.52	50.36	1.94
DOMINICA							
Crapaud soup	1172.8	92.88	26.04	14.88	288.2	144.16	19.8
Boogo (wilks) stew	6701	33.58	715	113.9	241.6	74.94	21.05
Rabbit 'Run-down'	2368	194.3	165.8	116.4	513.5	33.68	4.51
Plantain custard	1602	44.13	40.78	21.5	535.7	289.7	16.55
Tittiri accra	1247	103.6	3.81	0.39	0	194.3	7.31
GRENADA							
Oil down	3453	94.12	236.5	157.5	14.45	278.3	30.52
Pepperpot	3467.5	146.5	95.45	36.75	305.85	502	28.9
Cinnamon fried banana	267.9	1.33	8.27	5.01	20.71	51.49	1.94
Nutmeg ice cream	2276	38.25	160.2	95.03	1177	180.4	0
GUYANA							
Metagee	3869	121.4	107.5	60.51	0	630	29
Pepperpot	2146	214.2	115.4	22.22	2053	50.3	4.22
Cook up rice	3439	193.8	87.19	43.65	242.8	465.9	17.57
Gulgulla	1914	34.85	62.53	10.8	221.3	308.2	10.89
Cassava bread	658	5.443	1.4	0	0	159.2	0
Katahar curry	4608	61.33	146.28	105.64	0	560.4	104.23

Recipe	Energy kcal	Protein g	Total fat g	Saturated fat g	Cholesterol mg	Carbohydrate (total) g	Dietary fibre g
JAMAICA							
Rice and peas	3906	78.96	232.8	203.64	0	407	23.91
Sweet potato pudding	4682.4	45.48	248.28	207.36	0	614.76	19.8
Ackee and salt fish	773.4	42.03	63.48	7.8	165.18	8.91	1.73
MONTSERRAT							
Montserrat mixed marmalade	3475	4.87	2.54	0.219	0	898.6	14.04
Montserrat citrus marmalade	4962	6.35	0.89	0.116	0	1281	16
ST CROIX							
Maufe	4900.8	501.68	290.88	98.48	1508	35.08	3.54
Cowitch fish	3766	183.5	329.6	53.85	426.9	18.98	1.190
Sweet potato dumb bread	1023.2	20.32	39.52	8.72	16.48	146.08	8.91
Papaya nut cake	5124	103.3	237	41.02	639	661.1	24.24
Papaya pie	2499.2	22.95	115.84	34.312	31.064	348.88	15.51
ST KITTS AND NEVIS							
Conch fritters	1957	190.3	48.86	11.35	215.3	171.9	8.52
Escoveitched fish	1972	285.8	61.05	9.2	496.3	67.99	4.85
Stuffed avocado salad	1718	55.36	122.7	31.49	485.9	119.1	47.26
Rikkita beef	1872.4	42.48	159.68	34.48	153.36	31.16	2.48
ST LUCIA							
Labourer's lunch	19791	577.7	1265	280.3	993.1	1544	50.13
Stewed chicken dudon	5052.8	274.16	396.64	123.28	912	98.88	17.49
Cassava pone	2967	14.64	66.55	50.27	62.13	597.2	5.47
ST VINCENT AND THE GRENADINES							
Stuffed jacks	1997	149.6	111.4	23.22	320.2	90.51	4.05
Green banana mince pie	3728	114.8	182.4	63.02	623.6	445.2	11.35
Madungo dumplings	2018	23.97	93.51	51.51	15.9	284.7	33
SURINAME							
Nasi goreng	4759.57	88.6	70.26	23.39	673.5	499.92	1.14
Peanut soup	3887.06	214.04	187.19	1.19	900	390.81	20.58
TRINIDAD AND TOBAGO							
Bul jol	2241	413.2	43.37	7.532	985.8	30.79	8.29
Sancoche	2533	143	190.4	131	603.3	94.33	19.5
Trinidad peas and rice	3460	140.4	164	114.8	146.1	374	3.97
Pastelles	6839	297	249	85.4	737.7	884	123.5

Recipe	Minerals						Vitamins							
	Calcium mg	Iron mg	Potassium mg	Sodium mg	Zinc mg	Iodine	Vitamin A R.E	Thiamin mg	Riboflavin mg	Niacin mg	Vitamin D µg	Folacin µg	Cobalamin µg	Vitamin C mg
ANGUILLA														
Baked eel	220	5.86	2530	2651.2	14.91	0	9456	0	1.568	0.56	32.44	72.78	27.2	16.96
ANTIGUA AND BARBUDA														
Antigua Sunday morning breakfast	866.6	16.33	8680	32933	9.34	0	964.1	3.47	1.77	1.96	39.27	309.7	46.51	106.8
Antigua pepperpot	1805	75.18	12651	3151	34.36	0	5738	0	5.83	5.03	75.2	2021	2.95	704.3
Cornmeal – Fungee	36.38	11.54	545.5	542.8	2.15	0	131.6	0	2.01	1.14	14.16	145.9	0	4.95
BAHAMAS														
Conch chowder	181.32	17.95	3190.8	2879.4	35.67	0	4612.2	0.24	0.6	0.9	13.08	210.84	32.33	192
Chicken souse	245.7	22.93	3627	5175	28.03	0	2377	0	0.90	2.84	77.11	409.7	10.73	117.4
Johnny cake	252.42	10.122	311.76	4062.6	1.82	0	856.2	0	1.14	0.78	5.46	68.16	0.06	0
Guava duff	506.04	12.72	1783.2	3746.4	3.79	0	2173.2	14.16	1.44	1.56	16.86	159.18	1.08	833.4
Hard sauce	59.25	0.61	114.9	1935	0.23	0	1710	0	0.01	0.23	0.13	7.35	0.35	0
BARBADOS														
Flying fish melts in cheese sauce	931.7	8.14	585.7	1903	3.52	0	915.8	8.29	0.64	1.54	14.75	47.73	1.40	9.97
'Doved' peas	552.5	23.32	6294	1700	14.31	0	58.6	0	3.52	1.14	19.04	1892	0.78	92.26
Cou cou	82.18	11.69	645.5	4353	2.32	0	220.5	0	2.05	1.16	14.43	160	1.012	9.9
Jug-jug	4907	255.9	46981	844.3	94.01	0	1565	2.24	24.05	8.95	163.4	15064	0.03	56.1
Conkies	587	17.37	2732	1094	8.41	0	5347	2.87	1.14	1.93	9.35	329.9	1.44	123.7
BELIZE														
Arroz con pollo	2046	28.72	7059	2965.15	14. 3	0	11759	0	2.6473	2.35	73.76	255.57	0.904	122.42
Letu banana mulsa	24.5	3.91	1292	872.83	3.4	0	36	0	0.22	0.45	1.45	0	0	32
CAYMAN ISLANDS														
Zuppa di pesce	311.4	4.33	1626	960.1	5.86	0	282.2	0	0.19	0.26	5.7	65.33	8.58	47.93
Beer-batter fish	323.8	14.92	276.16	1541.2	1.08	0	136.32	0	1.24	1.88	30.44	59.28	0.08	5.2
Coconut cream pie	1158	7.79	1810	2797	6.13	0	2161	12.67	0.95	2.23	6.21	139.4	4.66	11.05
Banana mudslide	69.47	0.57	548.1	35.36	0.48	0	62.7	0	0.08	0.23	0.75	26.16	0.15	10.83

DOMINICA														
Crapaud soup	386.08	14.4	5156	1216.4	7.56	0	8984	0.2	1.72	1.92	17.64	322.2	1.84	149.36
Boogo (wilks) stew	346.5	43.6	1710	2350	174.2	0	516.5	0	0.71	0.52	8.02	110.3	73.64	44
Rabbit 'run down'	319.3	24.15	4416	6843	17.89	0	51.2	0	1.07	1.4	69.88	155.4	64.94	29.38
Plantain custard	1055	6.41	4622	564.6	5.00	0	1049	9.55	0.58	2.08	6.26	263.3	1.62	85.6
Tittiri accra	173.2	13.59	1501	683.6	1.76	0	79.58	0	1.21	1.62	15.91	65.7	0	23.18
GRENADA														
Oil down	649.5	36.52	4603	2380	6.59	0	4540	0	1.53	1.37	30.59	251.7	0.72	193
Pepperpot	471.95	44.75	3676	2249.5	21.7	0	775	0	3.6	2.85	41.05	342.95	13.15	168.45
Cinnamon fried banana	50.67	1.48	545.1	89.02	0.28	0	80.98	0	0.06	0.12	0.66	22.17	0.01	10.79
Nutmeg ice cream	749.8	2.61	1014	772.4	3.96	0	1927	14.59	0.32	1.75	0.59	100.2	3.45	5.51
GUYANA														
Metagee	1179	31.01	5085	1855	5.85	0	996.1	0.56	2.2	2.19	32.1	205.2	0.01	194.2
Pepperpot	500.1	17.63	2358	2642	31.64	0	223	0	0.509	2	29.1	35	16	19.62
Cook up rice	618.7	52.91	4680	449	16.28	0	563.5	0	3.98	1.7	54.87	1101	2.13	36.72
Gulgulla	291	11.36	1294	916.7	2.75	0	241	2.38	1.24	1.20	11.06	108.8	0.73	12.95
Cassava bread	178	3.2	0	4264	0	0	0	0	0.3	0.14	2.72	0	0	163.3
Katahar curry	1544.4	95.34	5504.4	4590	8.34	0	132.36	1.704	1.056	41.04	0	316.2	0	94.968
JAMAICA														
Rice and Peas	383.22	41.34	4467	4456	15	0	34.97	0	2.424	0.6	26.4	691.8	0	51.52
Sweet potato pudding	677.64	35.04	5187.6	1898.4	8.76	0	7936.8	1.49	1.176	0.78	18.96	231.72	0.012	73.2
Ackee and salt fish	169.83	3.3	1209	711	2.82	0	106.62	0	0.261	0.3	5.61	121.2	1.572	85.53
MONTSERRAT														
Montserrat mixed marmalade	150.9	3.035	1158	17.99	0.956	0	100.6	0	0.661	0.287	2.948	117.5	0	251.9
Montserrat citrus marmalade	259	1.549	1300	18.15	0.909	0	171.5	0	0.557	0.266	1.983	183.2	0	374.3
ST CROIX														
Maufe	492.56	22.3	4616	6185.6	31.6	0	343.76	0	8.544	4.304	76.632	93.76	16.32	39.28
Cowitch fish	247	12.59	3832	784.9	6.341	0	119.5	1.039	3.838	75.58	0	29.10	39.92	23.63
Sweet potato dumb bread	344.48	5.82	559.2	1727.2	1.84	0	4243.2	4.64	0.752	0.8	6.64	78.88	0.48	44.72
Papaya nut cake	901.2	33.22	3435.6	3009.6	10.43	0	391.92	1.8	2.4	2.4	21.84	365.16	1.56	135.48
Papaya pie	180.96	8.24	1656.8	1472.8	1.76	0	264	0	1.02	0.72	10.07	262.4	0.02	347.6
ST KITTS AND NEVIS														
Conch fritters	523.3	98.45	3930	3651	303.5	0	176.4	0.61	1.94	4.98	41.35	81.43	0.63	137.9
Escoveitched fish	939.1	7.93	6100	9405	5.21	0	1102	0	0.76	0.22	4.8	96.57	40.82	109
Stuffed avocado salad	720.9	11.44	5087	2555	9	0	1117	2.48	1.54	1.9	18.49	832	1.59	129.1
Rikkita beef	81.76	5.8	1021.2	1999.6	8.96	0	104.32	0	0.252	0.39	7.56	29.68	6.92	28.8

Recipe	Minerals						Vitamins							
	Calcium mg	Iron mg	Potassium mg	Sodium mg	Zinc mg	Iodine	Vitamin A R.E	Thiamin mg	Riboflavin mg	Niacin mg	Vitamin D µg	Folacin µg	Cobalamin µg	Vitamin C mg
ST LUCIA														
Labourer's lunch	1737	185.6	19100	3953	33.51	0	3682	0	13.08	7.68	131.3	3995	0.57	195.3
Stewed chicken dudon	451.44	17.2	3953.6	4420.8	26.96	0	2443.2	18.08	1.12	0.4	65.52	261.84	3.12	128.64
Cassava pone	542.5	13.2	1217	627.2	2.52	0	216.1	0	0.60	0.33	6.26	12.96	0.04	329.8
ST VINCENT AND THE GRENADINES														
Stuffed jacks	356.6	15.76	3048	3182	5.76	0	243.3	1.13	1.38	3.26	61.79	41.66	29.95	24.58
Green banana mince pie	532.2	23.38	1804	5771	18.26	0	1921	7.049	1.059	1.757	31.4	112.5	13.19	437.5
Madungo dumplings	254.3	10.83	3261	1908	3.28	0	227.1	2.26	1.09	0.53	8.83	165.2	0.02	24.74
SURINAME														
Nasi goreng	234.58	9.87	18402	4458.7	19.04	0	260.68		5.18	1.81	81.22	166.1	3.39	87.16
Peanut soup	49.08	21.77	2026.26	6876.18	1.87	0	393.62		0.46	0.21	10.96	100.20		39.12
TRINIDAD AND TOBAGO														
Bul jol	1078	18.26	10840	45619	11.29	0	518.1	0	2.072	1.874	53.21	289.3	64.87	88.3
Sancoche	1067	24.86	4686	4240	30	0	1274	0	1.22	1.223	29.36	413	35.1	201
Trinidad peas and rice	487.3	27.23	5812	2428	20.3	0	154	0	4.47	1.57	34.3	970.2	2.44	61.4
Pastelles	327	50.3	7085	2201	66.77	0	775	0	4.69	4.38	80.61	310	17.45	134

Fruit and vegetable recipes

Recipe	Energy kcal	Protein g	Total fat g	Saturated fat g	Cholesterol mg	Carbohydrate (total) g	Dietary fibre g
Apricot cheese	7727.3	17.69	2.16	0.147	0	1999.2	43.56
Apricot granola	3561.6	57.288	234.84	84.852	0	341.4	37.86
Apricot liqueur	3383.4	6.624	1.986	0.162	0	736.8	8.61
Avocado choka	313.1	5.6	31.11	0.037	0	10.3	26.28
Avocado shake	621	18.4	38.2	13.05	66	52	6.6
Black-eye punch	901.2	44.49	31.89	2.691	15.27	111.8	15.8
Boulanger cakes	1432	31.43	79.12	38.15	342	154. 2	1.811
Breadfruit surprise	911.5	18.1	17.51	10.21	66	174.4	0
Breadnut pudding	2350	18.89	99.8	20.53	215.2	350.1	0.204
Breadnut punch	871	14.34	14.24	8.113	51.3	157.1	0
Candied breadnut	1876	1.996	1.13	0.003	0	479. 3	0
Candied cashew apple	5993.8	17.7	2.73	0	0	1520.48	18.43
Carambola achar	443.6	10.24	6. 323	0.169	0	95.24	15.03
Cashew apple chutney	2125.7	12.7	2.8	0	0	543.64	16.41
Fat pork jam	1149	3. 272	1.05	0.007	0	298	6.787
Fat pork wine	7929	14.6	4.4	0. 051	0	2048	27.99
Ochro leaves, country style	1312	27	91.5	20.83	218	101.4	7. 35
Okracha	2545.6	198.08	115.04	38.448	633.92	185.52	16.344
Pickled breadnut	267. 3	3.43	1.731	0.011	0	59.92	0.68
Pineapple lamps	1461.8	34.38	59.64	7. 926	0	213.78	28.056
Plantain horns	1629	30.13	91.2	22.32	268. 2	190.8	12.3
Pumpkin liqueur	2327	9.612	1.061	0.483	0	470.1	15.64
Pumpkin nut fudge	1102	5. 894	27.82	7. 203	17	215	5.178
Pumpkin wine	6247	58.8	6.92	1.28	0	1564	59.59
Roasted pumpkin seeds	285	11.9	12.4	2.4	0	34.4	29.4
Stuffed baked pumpkin with pumpkin leaves	1993.2	145.16	111. 24	33.136	297.28	122.52	38.308
Sweet and sour apricot	1287	6.4	1.81	0.133	0	327. 2	8.609

Recipe	Minerals						Vitamins							
	Calcium mg	Iron mg	Potassium mg	Sodium mg	Zinc mg	Iodine	Vitamin A R.E	Vitamin D µg	Thiamin mg	Riboflavin mg	Niacin mg	Folacin µg	Cobalamin µg	Vitamin C mg
Apricot cheese	239.76	23.72	6688.5	73.353	4.116	0	3211.46	0	0.098	4.9	14.7	0	0	21.756
Apricot granola	332.4	22.116	2403	1626	14.784	0	172.56	0	1.44	1.2	12	148. 92	0	3.6
Apricot liqueur	188.22	5.88	1398.6	60.96	2.082	0	1186.8	0	0.18	0.192	3	39.07	0	47.364
Avocado choka	60.4	1.671	1425	653.1	1.91	0	20.79	0	0. 228	0. 376	4.596	18	0	31.56
Avocado shake	607.1	2.887	1271	249.6	2.358	0	222	5.1	0. 268	1. 243	2.12	94.12	1.742	15.92
Black-eye punch	803.1	4.875	1687	366.8	2.989	0	620.7	0	0.915	1.779	7.974	219.1	0.6	9.569
Boulanger cakes	441.4	12.89	1738	2249	3. 324	0	829	1.74	1.671	1.1	14.3	104	0.436	74.79
Breadfruit surprise	766	5.42	743. 3	629.6	1.9	0	184.4	5.1	0.187	0.791	0.414	24	1.742	4.58
Breadnut pudding	747.7	28.02	1174	5585	1.514	0	1287	11	0.128	0.498	4. 2	30.69	1.128	9.538
Breadnut punch	641.4	5.45	566	843	1.48	0	126. 3	3.938	0.13	0.595	0. 34	17.1	0.974	3.5
Candied breadnut	577. 2	13.97	1574	569	0.847	0	0.15	0	0.04	0.032	0.381	2.1	0	0.163
Candied cashew apple	776.34	25.88	1217.2	81.72	0	0	544.8		0.42	0.42	27.03	Tr	0	2982.9
Carambola achar	221.2	5.502	2031	576	1.788	0	608	0	0. 374	0. 342	4.519	102	0	206
Cashew apple chutney	311.8	15.78	383.3	1960	0.25	0	420.45		0.375	0.404	18.74	Tr	0	2030.6
Fat pork jam	91	1.01	366	70.42	0.099	0	0.013	0	0.03	0.55	0.181	0.11	0	65.22
Fat pork wine	1918	38.73	7808	1007	3.832	0	0	0	0.35	0.557	7.8	102	0.001	259.4
Ochro leaves, country style	241.8	9.143	764.4	2030	2.133	0	599.5	0.62	0.706	0.771	7.03	93.09	0.49	86.51
Okracha	471.52	24.832	6361.6	5096.8	34.656	0	1018.4	0	1.832	2.152	38.256	748.8	0	11.0880
Pickled breadnut	281. 2	7.743	62.75	582.9	0.076	0	0	0	0.02	0.01	0.059	7.6	0	2.55
Pineapple lamps	112.48	4.896	3120	930	4.746	0	37.71	0	0. 927	0.612	20.271	192	0	90.93
Plantain horns	531	7.4	2581	1548	3.685	0	790. 2	0.62	0.727	0.956	7.499	159	0.816	60.02
Pumpkin liqueur	205.9	7.775	159.1	15.1	3. 3	0	1455	0	0.5	0.02	5. 56	136.8	0	117.4
Pumpkin nut fudge	177	1.03	520	333	1. 22	0	460. 3	3.543	0.088	0.306	0.625	17.1	0.462	6.952
Pumpkin wine	1650	54.47	10452	782	14.2	0	1035	0	3.661	7. 221	53.68	2824	0.02	186.1
Roasted pumpkin seeds	42	2.12	588	1078	6.59	0	3.84	0	0.022	0.033	0.183	5.76	0	0.2
Stuffed baked pumpkin with pumpkin leaves	1519. 2	21.296	6084	4296	9.64	0	3781.6	1. 2	2.08	3.88	23.6	591.6	4.444	364
Sweet and sour apricot	319	8.3	2323	115.7	1.71	0	1185	0	0.166	0. 201	2. 972	40.4	0	45.69

Main dishes

Recipe	Energy kcal	Protein g	Total fat g	Saturated fat g	Cholesterol mg	Carbohydrate (total) g	Dietary fibre g
Beans in yellow boats	1708	59.1	81	31.23	173.2	194.4	18.1
Calypso peas	955.6	23.66	52.28	7.88	0	107	18.46
Chicken yammays	2201	1.97	77.1	22	535.4	171.2	16.2
Crunchy balls	2316	73	191	27.3	0	106.2	32
Farine pie	2310	67	144.2	40	564	192.1	1.03
Fish coubouillon	2115.6	241.2	116.88	19.32	426.9	14	0.636
Pigeon peas pinwheel	1914	29.2	49.4	9.237	0	347.6	3.72
Salt fish and vegetables in rice ball	1897	60.94	106.7	21	308.6	175.4	6.8
Shrimperi loaf	2244	51.4	125.2	19	551	226.9	6.7
Sweet salt fish cakes	3804	208.1	167.1	28	1013	375.6	16.7
Vegetarian roll	1424	60.78	68.26	38.1	134.3	153.6	39.6
Zesty legume loaf	2009	104.6	76.62	13.23	426	241	46.4

Carailli

Recipe	Minerals						Vitamins							
	Calcium mg	Iron mg	Potassium mg	Sodium mg	Zinc mg	Iodine	Vitamin A R.E	Vitamin D µg	Thiamin mg	Riboflavin mg	Niacin mg	Folacin µg	Cobalamin µg	Vitamin C mg
Beans in yellow boats	952.9	6.87	3491	2652	5.86	0	1500	4.54	0.52	0.8	4.5	233.4	4.963	63.2
Calypso peas	304.14	6.64	2024.4	3576	3.664	0	3637.2	2.25	0.72	0.512	5.76	423.2	0.03	168.4
Chicken yammays	261	10.84	5306	6898	8.1	0	602.3	0	0.894	0.994	56.85	161.6	1.423	79.4
Crunchy balls	222	11.01	2486	2649	10	0	313.5	2.24	1.4	0.4	32.2	674	0.03	5.131
Farine pie	855.3	8.722	1352	5708	9.2	0	1503	15.4	0.7	1.8	10.85	101	4.972	171
Fish coubouillon	411.72	2.75	4896	2121.6	4.2	0	918	4.54	0.552	0.96	3.68	69.5	31.86	54.88
Pigeon peas pinwheel	373.3	10.24	1239	2326	2.432	0	771.4	4.54	1.042	0.602	8.97	245	0.053	278.3
Salt fish and vegetables in rice ball	498.9	12.66	1268	1344	5.41	0	838.2	1.258	1.35	1.09	15.55	112	2.03	81.11
Shrimperi loaf	244	6.65	1045	1359	6.65	0	372	1.226	0.73	0.832	9.59	240.1	2.07	30
Sweet salt fish cakes	719.4	23.05	5616	3271	9.141	0	1052	4.11	2.7	2.62	37.24	306	8.841	85
Vegetarian roll	195	10.98	2716	943.3	7.11	0	754	0	1.4	0.5	7.2	455	0.034	42.14
Zesty legume loaf	562	25.42	3662	2575	12.11	0	322	1.226	2.24	1.6	27.56	934.8	1.12	15

Baked goods and sweet flavours

Recipe	Energy kcal	Protein g	Total fat g	Saturated fat g	Cholesterol mg	Carbohydrate (total) g	Dietary fibre g
BREADS, MUFFINS AND PANCAKES							
Bran sweet potato loaf	2850	76.64	113.7	24.73	246	402.2	20.3
Cheese cups	2080	71.3	73.02	21.2	478	280	6.2
Cinnamon lentil loaf	2302	63.34	111.3	24.74	246	271	9.22
Katy's breakfast muffins	2633.6	95.01	127.65	46.42	818.56	277.92	12.64
Nutty butternut squash loaf	1838	37.1	63.23	11	0	289	13.4
Nutty pumpkin bread	2845	61.7	111	38.2	337.1	396	22
Pineapple muffins	1756.8	39.99	58.78	12.53	426	266.6	8.68
Pineapple rolls	5311	162.7	84.55	20.1	459.1	964.8	44.5
Potato bread	2910	69.38	81.3	13.78	8	477.3	21.92
Pumpkin pancakes	940.3	14.31	33.65	6.7	17	145.4	6.34
Spinach nut loaf	2390	61.2	148.62	26.78	221.2	220	10.94
Tutti frutti loaf	2926	55.87	113.1	24	852	440.3	27.93
OTHER BAKED GOODS							
Black-eye buns	3753	132.12	104.13	19.13	0	592.65	134.37
Black-eye cookies	1845	26.433	93.69	19.43	0	229.59	19.58
Breadfruit caramel cake	2106	35.2	49.66	30.5	852	358.1	11.1
Breadfruit pastry	978.4	27.776	3.552	0.4	0	228.48	7.24
Breadfruit pizza (vegetarian)	3016.8	93.52	97.12	49.19	665.6	437.5	35.2
Breadfruit pone	1841	18.92	66.78	33.21	17	299.4	9.01
Golden apple 'n' cream sponge cake	2863	41.44	116.8	64	981.5	420.6	8.34
Hummingbird cake	4297	58.5	226	31.43	426	533.3	22.84
Nature's layered guava cake	4991	68.21	214.5	49	685.1	707.1	10.85
Guava icing	2422	0	75	15	0	457.2	0
Pineapple coconut bars	2464.8	26.1	123.8	37.3	426	325.3	10.84
Ripe breadfruit cake	1949	31.8	104.3	19.63	426	219.3	7.041
SWEET FLAVOURS							
Hibiscusade	815.9	1.027	0.465	0.036	0	211.3	0.399
Peppermint liqueur	3313	0	0.165	0	0	453.6	0
Peppermints	1840	6.25	5.093	1.55	213	454.2	0

Recipe	Minerals						Vitamins							
	Calcium mg	Iron mg	Potassium mg	Sodium mg	Zinc mg	Iodine	Vitamin A R.E	Vitamin D µg	Thiamin mg	Riboflavin mg	Niacin mg	Folacin µg	Cobalamin µg	Vitamin C mg
BREADS, MUFFINS AND PANCAKES														
Bran sweet potato loaf	1655	48.5	1726	5297	15.11	0	4719	15.7	1.53	3.3	121	399.1	6.7	85
Cheese cups	1908	4.99	992	3741	5.51	0	873.1	8.38	0.653	1.412	8.8	99.22	3.65	2.8
Cinnamon lentil loaf	1281	20.5	1608	2293	3.94	0	1307	12.24	0.5	1.432	70.34	343.4	1. 54	9.43
Katy's breakfast muffins	1445.69	17.79	1480.32	2480	9.824	0	3075.2	13.52	2.496	2.832	16.75	197.44	3.84	27.984
Nutty butternut squash loaf	812.2	15.5	1461	1661	3.75	0	609.4	4. 54	2.033	1.46	19.3	98.41	0.1	12
Nutty pumpkin bread	170.4	23	1258	2682	4.9	0	777	0.613	2. 51	2.19	24.42	268.1	0.632	12
Pineapple muffins	1199.4	14.17	936.2	2826	3.18	0	725.5	5.71	1.43	1.37	11.95	174.7	1.176	38.84
Pineapple rolls	605.8	55.06	2472	5080.8	13.22	0	822.5	8.26	9.89	7.97	94.32	971.5	1.2	50.26
Potato bread	229.4	24.97	2293	4037	6.24	0	461.6	4.524	3.236	3.004	36.01	727	0.278	28.16
Pumpkin pancakes	885.4	2.44	604	3991	2.05	0	179	1.275	0.303	0. 33	5	22.42	0.44	6.9
Spinach nut loaf	1242.4	21.5	1818.8	2050	5.45	0	2628	10.32	0.406	1.564	73.1	317.2	0.88	18.6
Tutti frutti loaf	1592	10.53	4222	2521	6.266	0	1346	9. 3	0.9	1. 52	15.1	369.3	2. 32	147.2
OTHER BAKED GOODS														
Black-eye buns	971.1	37.84	7542	2561.4	12.44	0	1755	9.05	2.025	2.268	21.28	1448.1	0.099	43.69
Black-eye cookies	248.94	9.09	1276.2	1606.5	2.331	0	1015.2	9.045	0.648	0.576	6.876	209.52	0.099	2.853
Breadfruit caramel cake	2262	32.94	3368	1856	4.2	0	387.7	2.45	0.54	1.343	7.1	117.2	2.24	13.4
Breadfruit pastry	247.2	15.024	268	4656.8	1.752	0	0	0	1.152	0.8	10.88	65.04	0	0
Breadfruit pizza (vegetarian)	2677	38.1	3610	7711	13.6	0	7802.4	2.35	1.67	2.38	14.68	755.3	3	621.9
Breadfruit pone	547.5	24.66	1070	2690	2.1	0	464	4.64	0.41	0.43	6.2	45	0.48	4.14
Golden apple 'n' cream sponge cake	782.9	15.5	1105	1863	3.7	0	1496	9.811	1.04	2.101	7.1	116.5	3	52.55
Hummingbird cake	391.4	20.8	3277	1926	7. 4	0	201	1.23	1.72	1.87	18	240	1.12	57
Nature's layered guava cake	2169	38.34	2618	4032	6. 33	0	2737	22.43	2.7	2.57	25	189.1	3	268
Guava icing	0	0.5	20	6.235	0	0	0	0	0	0	0	0	0	0
Pineapple coconut bars	566.6	11.8	1501.2	2787.6	2.93	0	1079.8	10.27	0.77	0.95	5.63	110.38	1.212	37.12
Ripe breadfruit cake	457.3	13.89	595.7	2953	2.333	0	1103	10.27	0.817	1.039	7.082	105.1	1.097	15.67
SWEET FLAVOURS														
Hibiscusade	43.08	0.869	129.8	5.461	0.145	0	2.125	0	0.027	0.029	0.281	6.645	0	24.13
Peppermint liqueur	4.549	0.992	33.07	6.823	0.616	0	0	0	0.048	0.002	0	0	0	0
Peppermints	29.54	0.992	69.07	69.81	0.686	0	95.2	0.613	0.031	0.256	0.037	23	0.5	0

Conversion tables

Note: Generally, in most metric measurements, use is made of multiples of five, whereby an approximation of 25 grams is used to represent 1 ounce. However, for the purposes of this book the Imperial measurements in the recipes submitted were converted to metric, and in the interest of accuracy, a direct conversion rate was used.

Imperial	Cups and spoons	Metric
Dry ingredients		
1 oz flour	¼ cup or 4 tbsp	28 g
1 oz sugar or fat	⅛ cup or 2 tbsp	28 g
4 oz flour	1 cup	113 g
4 oz sugar or fat	½ cup	113 g
8 oz flour	2 cups	227 g
8 oz sugar or fat	1 cup	227 g
Liquid ingredients		
⅛ pint	¼ cup	70 ml
¼ pint	½ cup	140 ml
½ pint	1 cup	280 ml
1 pint	2 cups	560 ml
1¾ pints	3½ cups	1 litre

1 tablespoon = 15 g or 15 ml

Oven temperatures

Mark/regulo	Celsius (°C)	Fahrenheit (°F)	Explanation
1	120–140	250–275	very slow
2–3	150–170	300–325	slow
4	180–190	350–375	moderate
5	200–220	400–425	hot
6–7	230–250	450–475	very hot

Index

Index

Macmillan Education
Between Towns Road, Oxford, OX4 3PP
A division of Macmillan Publishers Limited
Companies and representatives throughout the world

www.macmillan-caribbean.com

ISBN 978-1-4050-2659-8

First published 2006

Designed by Melissa Orrom Swan
Photographs by Michael Bonaparte
Illustrated by Raymond Turvey (Turvey Books)
Cover design by Melissa Orrom Swan
Cover photograph by Michael Bonaparte
Food styling by Wendy Rahamut

Printed and bound in Malaysia

2010 2009 2008
10 9 8 7 6 5 4 3 2